The Romanovs Under House Arrest

THE
ROMANOVS
UNDER HOUSE ARREST

FROM THE 1917 DIARY OF A PALACE PRIEST

The Diary of Archpriest Afanasy I. Belyaev

Translated from the Russian
by Protodeacon Leonid Michailitschenko

Historical Setting, Epilogue, and Persons of Interest
by Marilyn Pfeifer Swezey

HOLY TRINITY PUBLICATIONS
The Printshop of St Job of Pochaev
Holy Trinity Monastery
Jordanville, New York
2018

Printed with the blessing of His Eminence,
Metropolitan Hilarion, First Hierarch
of the Russian Orthodox Church Outside of Russia

The Diary of Archpriest Afanasy I. Belyaev © 2004 The Recovery Foundation
The Historical Setting, Epilogue, Persons of Interest
© 2018 Holy Trinity Monastery
Compilation © 2018 Holy Trinity Monastery

PRINTSHOP of
SAINT JOB of POCHAEV

An imprint of

Holy Trinity Publications
Holy Trinity Monastery
Jordanville, New York 13361-0036
www.holytrinitypublications.com

ISBN: 978-0-88465-454-4 (hardback)

Library of Congress Control Number 2017964187

The text of the diary of Fr Afanasy was prepared for publication by the Recovery Foundation (Vozrojdenie) in Washington DC. Published in the *Pravoslavnaya Rus'* nos. 3–4 (2004) and as "The Diary of Archpriest Afanasy I. Belyaev" in *Orthodox Life* Vol. 54. nos. 2– 3 (2004).

Cover: Photo: Photographer unknown, Nicholas and his daughters under arrest. Scan of photograph. ID: 1000297. Source: The Romanov Collection. Beinecke Rare Book and Manuscript Library, Yale University; Vector Crown: Royal crown vintage design vectors 02. Source: freedesignfile.com. License: creativecommons.org/licenses/by/3.0/us/; Vector Ornaments: Ozz Design. IDs: 70283098, 70283116, 70851109. Source: Used under license from Shutterstock.com.

Contents

Preface

You hold in your hands a remarkable document: the diary of Archpriest Afanasy Belyaev, rector of the Sovereigns' Feodorovsky Cathedral after the February Revolution, who was destined to provide spiritual nourishment to the last Royal Family during what was, in effect, house arrest in the Alexander Palace during the period March–August 1917.

Fr Afanasy's diary is valuable first of all in that it reveals how the members of the Imperial Family sustained themselves before they were sent into exile, first to Tobolsk and then to Ekaterinburg. They sustained themselves by faith in the good will of God, faith that helped them to endure all of their subsequent humiliation at the hands of the rabble and the burdens of exile, and to prepare themselves internally for their martyrdom.

The exemplary devotion to the Church shown by the last emperor and by his august family had never been called into question, not even by his enemies. Their piety is particularly underscored, however, in the memoirs of Archpriest Belyaev. It is impossible to read the diary entry made by Archpriest Afanasy after hearing the confessions of the tsar's children without being profoundly and sincerely moved: "Grant, O Lord, that all children be on as high a moral level as were the children of the former Tsar. Such was their lack of hatred, their humility, their submission to the will of their parents, unquestioning dedication to the will of God, purity of thought and complete ignorance of secular filth—both passionate and sinful—that I was astounded, and could not decide whether I, as a spiritual father, should remind them of sins perhaps unknown to them, and how I should incline them to repent of sins of which they were not aware…"

Here are the impressions recorded by the rector of the Feodorovsky Cathedral after the confession of Nicholas Alexandrovich himself: "Oh how inexpressibly fortunate I felt to have been made worthy through the mercies of God to become the intermediary between the Heavenly King and the earthly one. For next to me stood the one who was loftier than anyone else living on earth. He was even now the Anointed One given to us by God, one who for twenty-three years, by the law of royal succession, was our reigning Russian Orthodox Tsar. And now, the humble servant of God Nicholas, as a meek lamb, wishing good for all of his enemies, not harboring any offense, praying fervently for Russia's prosperity, deeply believing in her glorious future, on bended knees, gazes upon the cross and the Gospel, and in the presence of my unworthiness, relates to his Heavenly Father the hidden secrets of his long-suffering life, and, reduced to dust before the greatness of the Heavenly King, tearfully asks forgiveness for his transgressions, voluntary and involuntary...." Such was the sovereign emperor's peaceful state of mind shortly prior to his martyrdom.

Glory and honor to the Recovery Foundation (Vozrojdenie) in Washington, DC, which took upon itself the task of preparing for publication the diary of Archpriest Afanasy Belyaev, and to Protodeacon Leonid Michailitschenko for his excellent translation.

Archpriest Victor Potapov
Rector of the Russian Orthodox Cathedral of St John the Baptist
Washington, DC

The Historical Setting

The year 1917 was a milestone in Russian history. The revolution that began in February and intensified in October brought an end to the monarchy and the rule of autocracy. A reign of terror began that nearly wiped out the cultural, spiritual, and artistic development of Russia's thousand-year history over the next seventy years. With it came the genocide of millions of men and women—all ranks of clergy, monastics, and believers who became Russia's New Martyrs and Confessors of the twentieth century.

The radical political movement that triumphed in 1917 was already at large in Russia at the time of the great reforms of Alexander II in the 1860s and 1870s. The liberation of more than twenty million serfs in 1861 was followed by social, judicial, economic, and artistic reforms affecting nearly every sphere of national life. The future looked promising.

The only shadow in this era of reform was the political opposition to it by socialist revolutionary organizations. Their political agenda was the destruction of the monarchy and the abolition of autocracy. Almost immediately after the publication of the reforms, proclamations were published calling for regicide and advocating extreme socialist principles, foretelling a *Russian red, socialist republic.*

Alexander II survived seven assassination attempts. But on March 1, 1881, despite all protective measures, an eighth attempt was fatal. A bomb was thrown under the tsar's carriage en route to the Winter Palace by a member of the People's Will, one of the radical revolutionary groups. The tsar was rushed by sleigh to the palace, where he died without regaining consciousness.

His successor, Alexander III, tightened the hold on autocracy during his short reign of thirteen years. He died in 1894 at the age of forty-nine, the result of an injury he sustained during the derailment of the imperial train at Borki near Kharkov in 1888.

Nicholas II succeeded him to the throne. He was twenty-six years old. The early years of his reign were characterized by hopeful idealism. In 1898, the young tsar proposed an International Peace Conference to discuss the formal limitation of armaments. Nicholas II was the first world leader to propose such an idea and it was not met with much enthusiasm by other political leaders. Nevertheless, the conference was held in 1899 in The Hague. While it did not achieve an arms limitation agreement, the conference marked the beginning of formal peace efforts that led to the establishment of the Permanent Court of Arbitration at The Hague, the Geneva Convention, the League of Nations, and eventually to the United Nations in 1945.

Autocracy came under attack again in 1905. Russia's defeat in the war with Japan brought about a wave of strikes, demonstrations, and violence. Universities became centers of revolutionary organization and propaganda. With the intensification of political unrest by the socialist revolutionaries, Russia was on the verge of civil war.

A general strike of 120,000 workers led to a demonstration on January 9, 1905.[1] It was to be a peaceful procession to the Winter Palace to present a petition to the tsar calling for a Constituent Assembly. The tsar was in Tsarskoye Selo, out of the city. He knew nothing about the advance of thousands of demonstrators to Palace Square. The police did not interfere, but military guards who were untrained in controlling crowds began to fire point-blank at the advancing multitude. Altogether 200 were killed and 800 wounded on that day which came to be known as "Bloody Sunday."

Less than a month later, on February 4, the Governor-General of Moscow, Grand Duke Sergei Alexandrovich, uncle of Nicholas II, was assassinated when a bomb was thrown at his carriage by a terrorist.

Something had to be done.

Nicholas was unwilling in principle to relinquish autocratic power. "I don't hold to autocracy for my own pleasure," he said to his minister of internal affairs, Prince Sviatopolk-Mirsky. "I act in this sense only because I am convinced that it is necessary for Russia. If it was simply a question of myself, I would happily get rid of all this."[2]

As tsarevich, Nicholas had taken the oath of loyalty to the state and to the autocracy required of the heirs to the throne at the age of sixteen. The oath, established by the law of succession in 1797, took place in the Great Church of the Winter Palace before the cross and the Gospel, calling on God as a witness. It was not to be taken lightly.

With "nothing but new strikes, murdered policemen, Cossacks and soldiers, riots, disorders and mutinies," as he wrote to his mother, Nicholas understood that the "only way out would be to give civil rights, freedom of speech and press, and to have all laws confirmed by a State Duma—that, of course, would be a constitution."[3]

On October 30, 1905, the tsar issued a manifesto granting Russia its first constitution and a wide range of civil rights. Sergei Witte became its first prime minister. And it created the Duma, a parliament, which had the right of veto over all legislation and significant control over the budget.

Autocracy, however, was still in place. The tsar remained the final arbiter of all affairs of state. Although the Duma was established on the principle of constitutionality, in reality it had to operate in an uncertain coexistence with the principle of autocracy.

What may never have been understood in the Duma, however, was Nicholas's own understanding of his role which was more religious than political. He understood that he had inherited a profound responsibility before God for the welfare of his people. In keeping with the concept of the Byzantine emperors and Old Testament kings inherited with Orthodoxy in the tenth century, the sovereign was more than a political ruler. He was the anointed of God. The power of the autocracy was defined as "a selfless burden of service"[4] to the Russian people.

"God is my strength and gives me peace of mind," as he wrote to his mother on December 1, 1905. "So many Russians these days have lost that spirit. That is why they are so often unable to resist the threats and intimidations of the anarchists."[5]

The radical, revolutionary groups were not appeased by the constitution of 1905. Their political agenda to abolish the autocracy was unchanged. Nevertheless, following the revolution of 1905 with the granting of a constitution and the establishment of a State Duma, Russia entered a final period of remarkable economic, social, and artistic development, the culmination of its Silver Age.

One of the most successful government programs was the plan to create an agricultural middle class of independent farmers drawing on the peasantry and liberated serfs. Prime Minister Peter Stolypin brilliantly conceived the plan in 1906. Land belonging to the state, the Imperial Family, and the gentry was given to the government for redistribution through this program. It included tax cuts, purchasing credit, and technical advice. Altogether five million families took part in this program.

But Stolypin became the next victim of the radical revolutionaries. On September 1, 1911, he was fatally shot during an intermission of *A Life for the Tsar* at the State Opera in Kiev. Stolypin turned toward the imperial box where the tsar and his family were present, and made the sign of the cross. He was rushed to a nearby clinic where he died four days later. The loss of this great statesman was a major blow to the fragile balance between the autocracy and the new Duma constitution.

The assassin, Dmitry Bogrov, admitted his allegiance to the Socialist Revolutionaries requesting that they announce that the assassination was the beginning of a new wave of revolutionary terror.

Progress in Russia's development nevertheless continued. By 1913, Russia was able to supply the world with one quarter of its wheat, in spite of the primitive methods often still used by much of the peasantry. The crop that year was 200 million bushels greater than that of the United States.

The industrial revolution that took place in Russia between 1900 and 1913 closely resembled the growth that had taken place in the United States several decades earlier. Industrialists became a large merchant class. Many became wealthy and were patrons of the arts. Their support was an important factor in the cultural and artistic renaissance that became Russia's Silver Age. Developments in painting, literature, and music directly influenced theatre, ballet, and the decorative arts. From the jeweled art of Fabergé to the Cubist paintings of Vrubel, Russian artists were in the vanguard of European art.

Many contemporary observers, both Russian and foreign, noted the transformation taking place in Russia. In 1913, a French journalist, Edmond Théry, investigating the Russian economy and Russia's remarkable success in other areas, wrote that if nothing changed in the next few years, by the middle of the century "Russia will dominate Europe politically, economically and financially."[6]

Gilbert Grosvenor was an American who traveled extensively in Russia in 1914. He dedicated the November issue of the *National Geographic* to "Young

Russia: Land of Unlimited Possibilities." He described Russia as a "youth among the nations ... because she never had a chance to grow until recent years."[7]

Russia was on the way to becoming a world superpower had war not intervened. As Prime Minister Witte noted in a conversation with cabinet member, Prince Volkonsky, "Russia will become a great world power ... unless there is a war."[8]

War clouds were rising from Germany. While Russia endeavored to remain on good terms with everyone, Germany's aggressive policy toward Eastern Europe and the Balkans brought about a growing danger of war. As Dominic Lieven pointed out, war was still widely regarded as honorable in pre-1914 Europe.[9] Noblemen were brought up to defend their honor at all cost. Russia had deep historical links to the Balkans and a commitment to the Franco-Russian alliance forged by Alexander III. This sense of honor was ultimately an important factor in drawing Russia into the war in 1914.

Nicholas loathed war, as Foreign Minister Sergei Sazonov recorded in his diary, and did everything he could to avoid it. But in the end, war was inevitable.

On the evening of August 1, 1914, the German ambassador in St Petersburg presented a declaration of war to Foreign Minister Sazonov. The next day, following a prayer service in the Winter Palace, Nicholas appeared on the balcony. An enormous crowd had gathered in the square and when he appeared, thousands knelt and sang the imperial hymn.

The war began with much optimism and the expectation that it would not last long. The name of the capital city was changed from the Germanic St Petersburg to the Slavic Petrograd. Things went reasonably well in the first nine months. However, by mid-1915, military setbacks and supply shortages began to confirm the dire predictions of Peter Durnovo, governor-general of Moscow. He had foreseen that in the event of war there would be an insufficiency of military supplies, inadequacy of strategic railways, expenditures beyond Russia's financial means, and that blame would be laid on the government. Russia would be flung into hopeless anarchy.

Although the military situation began to improve after Tsar Nicholas assumed supreme command in September 1915 and into 1916, the economy emerged as the most basic problem. Food supplies to the cities were drastically reduced as a result of concentration on the war effort.

Hostility toward the government began to develop, workers began to be influenced by socialist forces, and the Bolsheviks became a dominant force culminating in the arrival of Vladimir Ilyich Lenin in a sealed railroad car from Germany in April 1917.

Revolution began in Petrograd on Sunday, February 27, 1917, as Fr Afanasy noted in his diary. Serious disturbances were taking place throughout the city. Michael Rodzianko, president of the Duma, organized a temporary or Provisional Committee of the Duma to take responsibility and form a new government. He sent a message to the tsar attributing the disorders to "complete distrust of the government."[10] A soviet, or council, of workers and soldier deputies was formed and quickly made its way into the Provisional Committee of Duma politicians. The plan was to get Nicholas to abdicate in favor of his son.

The tsar was at Stavka, the military headquarters in Mogilev, when he learned that the government had lost control. He set off to return to Tsarskoye Selo. He ordered General N. I. Ivanov to command a special force to restore the authority of the government in Petrograd, but he was unable to get to Petrograd.

The imperial train was diverted to Pskov, arriving on March 1. That evening General Nicholas Ruzsky arrived and began to pressure Nicholas to concede to parliamentary rule and abdicate in favor of his son. Nicholas stated that he could not consider that he would not still be responsible before God even if he was no longer responsible before the people.[11] The Russian Coronation was, in fact, a sacrament, permanent in nature, bearing responsibility to God in service to the Russian people.

General Alekseev sent a request to all the military commanders to wire the tsar about abdication. They all agreed with the conviction of Rodzianko that the only way to save the dynasty was for the tsar to abdicate in favor of his son with regency to Nicholas's brother, Grand Duke Michael.

Abandoned by his generals, and after many hours of discussion with Ruszky, Nicholas agreed to do this. But after consulting Dr Feodorov, the family's surgeon, he decided not to abdicate in favor of Alexei because of his incurable illness, but directly to Grand Duke Michael.

Although this was not legal according to the law of succession, the deputies of the Provisional Committee of the Duma, Alexander Guchkov and Vasily Shulgin, who had arrived from Petrograd to get the abdication, accepted it.

At 11:40 p.m. on March 2, Nicholas II, seventeenth tsar of the Romanov dynasty, signed the Manifesto of Abdication. He wrote in his diary, "All around me is treason, cowardice and betrayal."[12]

Grand Duke Michael was advised by the Duma Committee not to take the throne as they could not guarantee his safety. He abdicated the next day

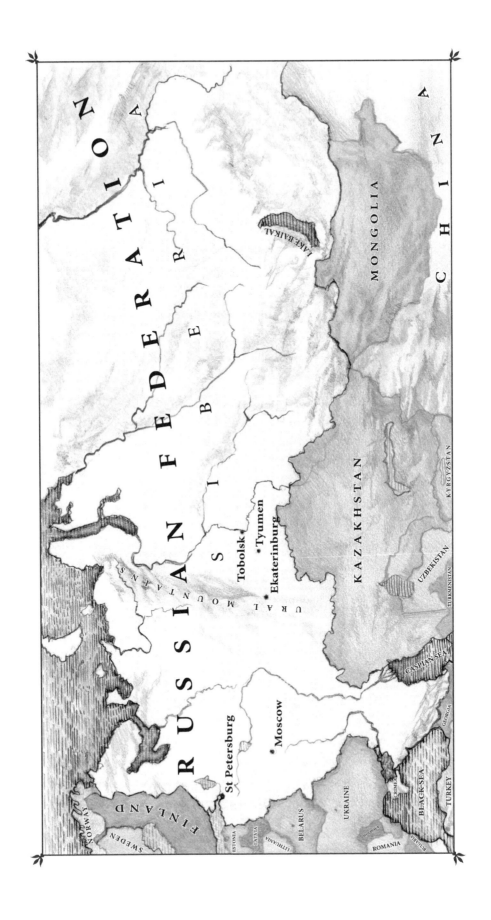

saying that he would assume the throne only after a decision of the upcoming Constituent Assembly. The monarchy was gone. The Provisional Government was in charge.

From Pskov, Nicholas headed back to Stavka[13] to take leave of the troops. In his last address he bade them to support the new authority. "May God help it to lead Russia along the road to glory and prosperity..."[14] The Provisional Government did not allow this to be published.

On March 4, his mother, Dowager Empress Marie Feodorovna, arrived at Mogilev having learned of the abdication. She spent four days during which time they spent many hours together. This was their last meeting.

The Petrograd Soviet acted quickly, directing the Provisional Government on March 7 to arrest the Romanovs. A letter was sent to Empress Alexandra at Tsarskoye Selo on March 8, informing her that she and the former tsar were under arrest. The children were never formally arrested but they remained with their parents and shared the conditions of their arrest.

On March 9, Nicholas, now the former tsar, returned to Tsarskoye Selo as to another world. Rough and rude guards replaced the courtiers. As his motor car approached the gate, the guard asked who was in it. "Nicholas Romanov," the sentry shouted out. The palace was without electricity and water, and the children were recovering from severe cases of measles. The family lived under house arrest in the Alexander Palace for five months.

It was the beginning of a restricted life. Telephone lines were cut. Incoming and outgoing letters were read. Everyone except Alexandra rose early. Nicholas and one of his entourage would walk for an hour and a half in the park. Lunch was at one o'clock, work in the garden until three when the children had their lessons, tea at four, dinner at seven. And so it was, day after day.

Alexander Kerensky, socialist head of the Provisional Government initiated a Special Investigative Committee to look into clandestine activities of former ministers, high ranking officials, and the former ruler. This committee was to publicize the "truth" of their activities and expose treasonous contacts with enemies of the state. The goal was to bring them to trial.

The anti-Romanov hysteria of the Russian press was spread through a myriad of revolutionary pamphlets and journals. The former empress and her sister, Grand Duchess Elizabeth, were accused of being German spies and attending to a clandestine visit of their brother, Grand Prince Earnest of Hesse, to negotiate a separate peace. Other false accusations were published along with the antimonarchist rhetoric of political leaders in the Duma as well as in America and Britain.

Many high officials were interrogated and interviewed. The former tsar was asked to turn over all his papers. He unhesitatingly complied with this request. In the end, after an extensive search, nothing incriminating could be found. The Special Investigative Committee was unable to prove any criminal deeds or contacts with the enemy in its investigation and eventually the plan fell through.

Kerensky came to the Alexander Palace on March 21 to inspect the rooms, "talk to Nicholas Alexandrovich,"[15] and announce that the palace had passed into his ministry as General Procurator. He described his impressions of the former tsar in his memoir later published in exile.

> I had been looking forward to the interview with the former Tsar with a certain anxiety, for fear of losing my temper when I came face to face with him… My first glimpse of the scene as I went up to the former Tsar changed my mood altogether.
>
> A small man in uniform moved forward to meet me… It was Nicholas II… I went up to him, held out my hand with a smile and said abruptly, "Kerensky," as I usually introduce myself. He shook my hand firmly and smiled.
>
> When I told him that Alexandra Feodorovna might have to be tried, he merely remarked: "Well, I do not believe that Alix had anything to do with this. Is there any proof?" To which I replied: "I do not know yet."
>
> In the course of my occasional visits to Tsarskoye Selo I tried to fathom the former Tsar's character. Nicholas, with his fine blue eyes and his whole manner and appearance, was a puzzle to me… I was struck by the fact that nothing about him suggested that only a month before so much had depended on his word… This indifference to all external things was almost unnatural. Power simply fell from his hands. He shed his authority as formerly he might have thrown off a dress uniform and put on a simpler one… a strange, awesome and yet disarming personality.[16]

During their time under house arrest the family and members of the household planted a large kitchen garden near the palace and kept up each other's spirits. The girls answered notes from well-wishers describing in a few words their activity and approach to their new life. In one of these notes, Grand Duchess Olga wrote:

July 12, 1917
Dearest Vera Vladimirovna,
    I am deeply touched and grateful to you for your good wishes. Our vegetable garden is flourishing. We helped to harvest hay and I have learned a little, how to scythe.
Wishing you all the best, O[17]

In what was perhaps his last letter from Tsarskoye Selo, Nicholas described their life in these simple words to his mother:

Tsarskoye Selo, July 1917
My dearly beloved Mama,
    An occasion has finally arisen to write you a few lines… I have not received any news from you since Mogilev… How terribly difficult it is to be cut off from one's own! … We are all healthy and in good spirits. All that is going on around us, however, is beyond description… The summer has been incredibly hot; we work in the vegetable garden with our dear people… We are giving lessons to the children and I am working with Alexis on Russian history and geography…
    I am constantly with you in thought and prayer. Christ be with you, my dear Mama, With boundless love,
        Your Nicky [18]

The presence of Fr Afanasy in the palace for all the services of Holy Week and Pascha, as well as the regular Saturday and Sunday services thereafter, was a great consolation for the family and all those who loyally remained with them.

As Count Paul Benckendorff, Marshall of the Court, later wrote, "Fr Belyaev deserves our most profound gratitude for all that he did for us with so much heart and soul. His words for us were a true comfort and consolation."[19]

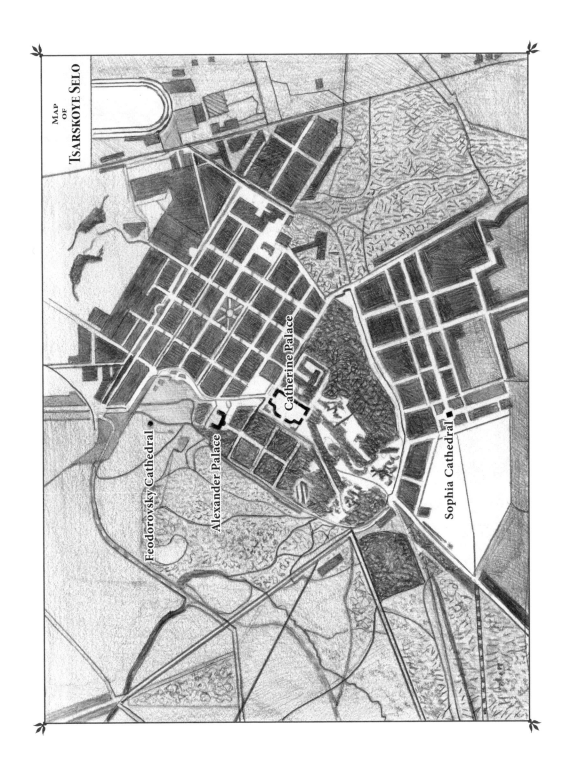

MAP
OF
TSARSKOYE SELO

Feodorovsky Cathedral •

Alexander Palace

Catherine Palace

Sophia Cathedral ▪

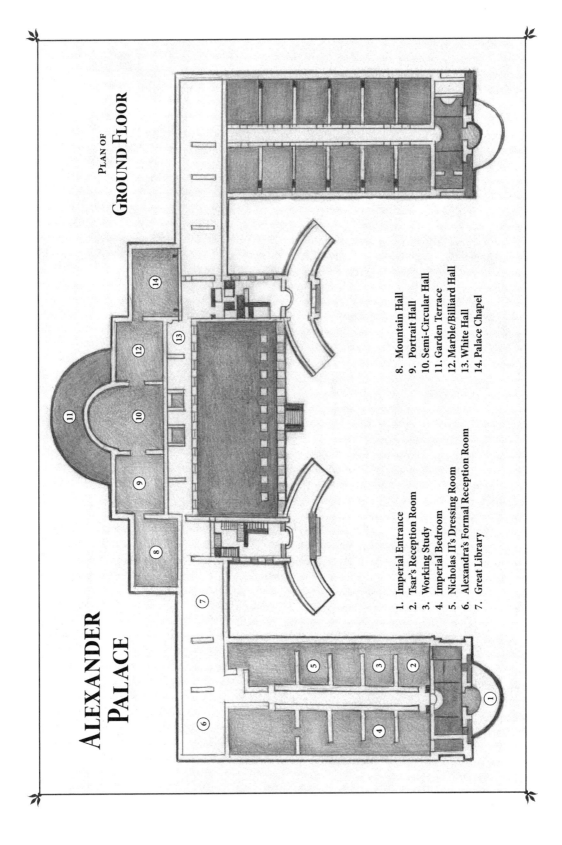

ALEXANDER PALACE

PLAN OF
GROUND FLOOR

1. Imperial Entrance
2. Tsar's Reception Room
3. Working Study
4. Imperial Bedroom
5. Nicholas II's Dressing Room
6. Alexandra's Formal Reception Room
7. Great Library

8. Mountain Hall
9. Portrait Hall
10. Semi-Circular Hall
11. Garden Terrace
12. Marble/Billiard Hall
13. White Hall
14. Palace Chapel

The Diary of Father Afanasy

Mitred Archpriest Afanasy Ioanovich Belyaev was the chaplain and confessor to Nicholas II and his family in the Alexander Palace during the period of their house arrest. (See Appendix 1 for his biography.)

March 2, 1917 ~ Dmitry Nikolaevich Lohmann, churchwarden of the Feodorovsky Cathedral, visited me and told me that I had been invited to come to the Znamensky Church, to take the miraculous icon of the Queen of Heaven[20] to the Alexander Palace and to serve a moleben [prayer service] in the children's wing of the palace, where the Tsar's children lay sick with measles. An automobile was provided, and took me to the Znamensky Church. Upon entering the church, I met its rector, Archpriest John F. Speransky, who had already arranged for vestments to be prepared, the icon to be brought, and personnel assembled to carry it. I immediately vested, took the cross, and to the singing of the troparion "As thou art an unassailable fortress and a fountain of miracles," departed, along with the clergy of the Znamensky Church, for the palace.

Despite the fact that the palace was guarded by sentries of the Combined Infantry Regiment, entry was unimpeded. From the entranceway, we ascended to the children's wing on the second floor. We passed a number of brightly lit rooms, and entered a large, dimly lit room, in which the sick children lay in their individual beds. The icon was placed on the table prepared for it. It was so dark in the room that I could barely make out who was present: the Empress, in the uniform of a Sister of Mercy, stood next to the Heir's bed. Near her stood other

15

Sisters of Mercy and children's nurses. Several slender wax candles were lit before the icon. The moleben began… Oh, what horrible and unexpected misfortune had befallen the Imperial Family!

Word had come that while, at the request of the Empress, the Sovereign was rushing to be with his family in Tsarskoye Selo, he was detained and arrested, and even that he had renounced the throne. Awful events are taking place in Petrograd: houses are being burned and destroyed, troops have betrayed the Tsar and, together with a mob of workers, are laying siege to police headquarters. They are arresting and replacing their superiors and former government officials, releasing criminals from prison, and, having proclaimed a republic, are proclaiming freedom for all. Rifle shots are ringing out on the Nevsky [Nevsky Prospekt, a street in St Petersburg], and there are innocent victims. There is a fierce battle taking place between the troops and the police. Nor is it calm in Tsarskoye Selo. In the Sophia District, where the troops are quartered, there is an uproar, savage cries, and ever more frequent rifle shots; soldiers storm and break up wine shops and stores, set fire to police stations, and release the imprisoned.

Can one imagine the state in which the helpless Empress, a mother with five grievously ill children, found herself? Suppressing her womanly weakness and all of her human ills, she heroically, selflessly, devoted herself to caring for the sick. Placing all of her reliance on the Queen of Heaven, she decided that the first thing to be done was to pray before the Icon of Our Lady of the Sign; thus, she directed that the icon be brought to the sick children's quarters. On her knees, tearfully, the earthly queen implored the help and intercession of the Queen of Heaven. After venerating the icon and passing underneath it, she asked that the icon be taken to the children's beds, so that they might also venerate the miraculous icon. As I offered her the cross, I said, "Take courage and be strong, Your Majesty; the dream may be frightening, but God is merciful. In all things, rely on His holy will. Believe, hope, and pray without ceasing." We carried the holy icon to all of the children's rooms, and then descended to a separate isolated room where Anna A. Vyrubova lay, covered with a rash, and sick with measles. There, while I read only the prayer before the icon of the Mother of God, the sick one inclined her fevered brow to the holy icon, and for a long time would not release it from her grasp. The Empress, who had descended via the interior staircase from the children's rooms, stood at the sickbed and also prayed fervently. By the time we had left the palace with the icon, the palace was already ringed with troops and all of the people within were under arrest.

March 11 and 12, 1917 ~ Saturday and Sunday. After the Sovereign came from headquarters to Tsarskoye Selo on March 9, I received a telephone call from the palace, summoning me to come to the Alexander Palace and, together with the protodeacon, chanter, and a choir of four, to serve the all-night vigil and the festal liturgy in the palace church. Upon our arrival at the palace, we were met by the commandant and a security guard. As I entered the first floor corridor leading to Their Majesties' quarters, the Sovereign's valet approached me and said, "His Majesty requests that you go to his room. He wishes to say a few words to you about the services to be done in the palace church." In response to these words, our young escort said, "Be so kind as to proceed to the church. You may not speak with him." The astounded valet said, "Excuse me, I will relay this to His Majesty." However, our stern escort answered, "It's all the same to me. I cannot permit any meetings with anyone, or any form of communication [with him]." And thus, without stopping, we went under escort and in total silence to the church.

Several minutes later, before the beginning of the service, Marshal of the Imperial Court Benckendorff entered the nave and, on behalf of the Sovereign, asked that I perform the services in the palace church on Sundays and feast days. After the vigil, I requested the palace commandant to indicate whether there were any orders for us with respect to serving the divine services, and as to how we were to behave toward the Sovereign—e.g., how were we to respond to any questions he might ask, and how were we to address him? How were we to commemorate him during services, and in general, how were we to behave toward all of those serving at the palace? The commandant replied, "There are no orders. Of course, one should respond to the Sovereign's questions, but the conversation must be of a nonpolitical nature, and in the presence of the guard. It would be best to avoid addressing him by title, although I personally call him 'Your Majesty.' Decline to meet with him in his quarters, and in general, the fewer opportunities for a rebuke from the guard, the better it will be for those under arrest."

And truly, the Sovereign and his spouse were so tactful and noble that they would appear at services after we were already standing vested in the altar, and they would be the first to leave the church after services… They stand in church totally apart, behind screens, occupying a little space in a corner with a separate entrance. When at the great entrance I was required, for the first time in the presence of the Sovereign, to commemorate not the "Pious Autocrat and Emperor" etc., but instead the "Russian Authorities and the Provisional Government," I at first could not bring myself to do so, and barely kept from bursting into tears… With my voice breaking, and stumbling over the words, I completed the commemorations…

March 24 and 25, 1917 ~ I served the vigil and liturgy, and again the vigil on the eve of Sunday. At the vigil, I distributed blessed branches of pussy willows, a single bare twig per person. Even in this, the arresting authority showed their disrespect.

March 27, 1917 ~ Nine a.m. Summoned by telephone, I arrived at the Alexander Palace to serve in the palace church throughout Passion Week and on the first two days of Pascha [Easter celebrations]. A room was prepared for me, on the highest floor of the palace, with a window looking down upon a small private garden. One could describe the room as luxurious, with all of the conveniences—constituting guestroom, office, and bedroom—airy, warm, comfortable, remarkably tidy, with a gilded bed with fine, snow-white sheets and a pale blue silk blanket. There is a servant, attentive and absolutely discreet. Next to the room is a corridor and a staircase going down directly into the church. The only negative feature is that the room is isolated; at the same time, this ensures that it is quiet.

I prepare to serve the Liturgy of Presanctified Gifts scheduled to begin at 11:00. I serve the liturgy. At each hour, I read the Gospel according to John, completing three chapters. The following were present and fervently praying at the liturgy: the former Emperor Nicholas Alexandrovich, Alexandra Feodorovna, Olga Nikolaevna, Tatiana Nikolaevna, and all those living near them, Naryshkina, Dolgorukova, Gendrikova, Buxhoeveden, Dolgorukov, Botkin, Derevenko, and Benckendorff. Standing apart and engrossed in a prayer book were many servants preparing themselves for confession. The liturgy ended at 12:30 p.m.

At one o'clock, tea and lunch were served for the three of us—myself, the protodeacon, and chanter. A wonderful lunch! Tea in silver teapots, and rolls, both brought on a silver tray. Then we were served rice cutlets with white mushrooms, cooked pike with potatoes, and for dessert, pancakes with jam, and finally, coffee. Thus, Great Monday turned out to be a day spent in palatial luxurious surroundings, in comfort, and replete with an abundance of excellently prepared foods.

At 4:00 p.m., a messenger arrived and announced that Their Majesties would commune not on Thursday, but on Saturday, and that the schedule was to be amended so that on Thursday the liturgy would be served not at 9:00 a.m. but at 11:30 a.m., and on Saturday at 9:30 a.m. rather than at 11:30 a.m.. At 8:00 p.m., after serving compline and matins, I returned to my room. Dinner was served: cabbage soup with mushrooms, accompanied by pirozhki, followed by cooked pike, and a baked apple with a sweet syrup, and then black coffee. At 10:00 p.m., tea was offered, but I declined. Prince Dolgorukov came by and asked me whether I was satisfied with the room and cuisine. At 10:00, I read the prayer rule for Holy Communion, and Dmitry of Rostov's instructions on preparing for confession. It is unusually quiet in the palace. I sit alone. Thus I spent my first day of life and service in the Alexander Palace, where the Royal Family is under arrest.

March 28, 1917 ~ I slept for four hours. I got up at 6:00 a.m., spent considerable time in thought. I read the morning prayers and Dmitry of Rostov's book. Quiet all around. I learned that Apraksin and Dolgorukov had occupied my room before me, and that upon my departure, it was to be given to Dr Botkin, now living in the children's quarters. At 10:00, services began—the hours and the reading of the Gospel. Nicholas Alexandrovich sent word that he would arrive for the beginning of the liturgy at 11:00, and this he did, along with Olga Nikolaevna. The service ended shortly after noon. At 1:00 p.m. I had some tea, and ate lunch: potato cutlets with a mushroom sauce, cooked pike, fruit compote, and a cup of coffee. After lunch, I lay down on a little couch, and read the works of Dmitry of Rostov. At 5:00, after tea, I went to church to serve the great compline and matins. The service, which lasted until 7:30, was attended by Nicholas Alexandrovich and his spouse, Olga and Tatiana Nikolaevna, and by all those preparing for confession. At 8:30, dinner was served: mushroom soup, fried smelts, and kissel [a fruit jelly]. I lay down to sleep at midnight.

March 29, 1917 ~ Arose at 7:00 a.m., prayed to God, and read the prayer rule for Holy Communion. I am waiting for the liturgy. It turns out that next to my room are [Catherine] Schneider's rooms, and on the other side are Vyrubova's servants, who are yearning for freedom. Three persons attended the liturgy. For the last time, great prostrations were done. After liturgy, I read the prayers for those preparing for confession, and gave some brief instructions on how to approach [the mystery of] repentance. Confession for the servants was scheduled for 2:00 p.m. At 1:00, lunch was served: sliced cabbage with pickles and potatoes, fish and kissel. Confessions began at 2:00 and continued until 5:00 p.m.. All told, fifty-four people came to confession. The remainder put off confession until Saturday. At 6:30, I began to serve matins with the festive hymn "The glorious disciples were illumined…." All of the services are sung by four soloists from the palace choir, dressed in purple robes. The service ended by 8:00 p.m.

…Today the palace commandant visited me at 5:00 p.m. He turned out to be a wonderful, quite humane and noble man. He announced that I was a free man, that I might freely wander throughout the palace halls and talk with anyone living in the palace, and might even go out into the garden to get a breath of fresh air. After vigil, I met and spoke with Botkin. Dinner was served at 8:00 p.m.: mushroom soup, fish, dry biscuits in a sweet syrup, and pieces of pineapple. I received a newspaper, the *New Times*.

March 30, 1917 ~ Wandered through the halls of the palace. I was amazed at how rich and luxurious it was. I looked out the windows of the Semi-Circular Hall, and watched as graves were being prepared for the victims of the siege upon the wine shops of Tsarskoye Selo. A site in an open field opposite the palace had been chosen as the cemetery. The liturgy, at which the Imperial Family and all of the communicants fervently prayed, ended about noon. Those who had prepared through confession modestly approached the holy chalice; to each I uttered a few words which could also be heard by everyone else in the church. After the liturgy, a messenger advised me that their spiritual father had sent word through Anitchkov that despite his ill health, he was willing to come hear the confessions of Their Majesties. However, he had been told not to trouble himself to come, as everything could be done without him. But no one knew who would be appointed as confessor in the spiritual father's stead, and orders in that regard have not yet been issued.

Apparently, things are going smoothly, and everyone has found the services satisfactory. From the Feodorovsky Cathedral, they have brought a small but excellent epitaphion [a shroud with a depiction of the dead Christ],[21] as well as a special table to hold it, a large book of the Gospels, and Paschal vestments. The altar table and the table of prothesis have been covered in black, and black vestments have been prepared for the clergy. The all-night vigil with the reading of the Gospels has been scheduled for 6:00 p.m. At 1:00, lunch was served: rice cutlets with white mushrooms, fried smelts, and fruit compote. At 4:00 p.m. I opened the window and heard martial music; they are playing the Marseillaise and funeral marches. Through the window I see many soldiers. Because of the great distance, I cannot make out what is being done at the gravesites, although this is all near the palace, opposite the Semi-Circular Hall, not far from the church. And this, on Great Thursday in Passion Week! Truly they know not what they do.

At 6:00 p.m., the service, with the twelve Gospel readings, began. The same faithful attended— a total of about 100 people with their retinues and servants, accompanied by the guards. The choir—the four palace choir soloists—sang beautifully, especially the "The Wise Thief."[22] The service was sung with piety and tenderness, but was somewhat abbreviated. The entire service lasted one hour and forty minutes. Their Majesties stood listening throughout the service. Folding analogia [lecterns], each holding a book of the Gospels, were placed before them, so that they might follow along throughout the readings. They all remained for the entire service, and departed for their rooms through the main entrance, something that they had not done heretofore.

One must really be this near to the former Royal Family, must see for oneself, in order to comprehend just how fervently—often on their knees—in what an Orthodox manner, the former Royal Family prays to God. With what obedience, meekness, and humility do they stand during divine services, giving themselves over entirely to the will of God. And in me, a sinful and unworthy servant at the altar of the Lord, my heart becomes still, tears pour forth, and despite the oppressive weight of confinement, the grace of the Lord fills my soul, and words of prayer flow out easily, touching and penetrating the listening faithful.

At 8:00 p.m., dinner is served: cabbage soup with mushrooms, roast [vegetables], and raspberry jelly. Nine p.m.: preparing for Friday. The epitaphion will be brought out into the church. I consider what I will say at the tomb of the innocent victim—our Saviour. I read in Russian translation the wonderful stichera [hymns] appointed for Great Friday, and draw comfort from their content. What will tomorrow bring? How many, and who, are preparing for confession…

March 31, 1917 ~ Nine a.m. I got up early, after spending a troubled night. I am in wonderful surroundings with all of the comforts—it is clean, light, warm, comfortable, and quiet, and yet, I cannot sleep. For a long time I pondered, and I splashed cold water on my head, then prayed to God and began to write a homily for the bringing out of the epitaphion. At noon, I went to the church and confessed those preparing for Communion. Forty-two came to confession, including two physicians, Botkin and Derevenko. At 1:30, I received word that I was to come at 5:30 to the children's quarters and prepare the three ill Grand Duchesses and the former Heir for Communion. At 2:00 p.m., vespers, with the bringing of the epitaphion into the center of the church, began. The place for the epitaphion was covered with carpets, and bouquets of blooming red and white lilacs and a multitude of roses were brought to make a marvelous and elegant bed of live flowers. Surrounded by this curtain of flowers was the table for the epitaphion, brought from the Feodorovsky Cathedral. Their Majesties, two Grand Duchesses, and their retinue arrived in deep mourning—all attired in black dresses. Vespers was conducted with appropriate decorum and pomp. The epitaphion was brought into the center of the church. I gave a homily.

> What a sad, solemn, spiritual event is now being marked in all
> Orthodox churches! The bringing out of the epitaphion. Before
> us is the tomb, bearing the holy depiction of the Divine Sufferer,
> One Who died for the sins of all mankind. Oh, how powerfully

and irresistibly am I, a sinner, drawn to this tomb, and to wash His most-pure body not with sweet-smelling myrrh, but with the tears of repentance. Oh, how clearly I hear His final words, spoken from the Cross. I hear that soul-rending cry, uttered just before His death, asking His Heavenly Father, "My God, My God, why hast Thou forsaken Me!" What depth of despair is heard in that cry! "Even though people may have left Me, even though friends and acquaintances may have abandoned Me. Even though relatives and those close to Me may have abandoned Me! But Thou, My Heavenly Father, why hast Thou become so angry with Me? For what reason hast Thou turned Thy marvelous, glorious, loving gaze away from Me?" And what an awesome, unique event. From the heavens, neither voice nor hearing. From the heavens from which on more than one occasion were heard the words of the Heavenly Father "This is My Beloved Son, heed Him," there now is not a sound. A horrible state… To feel, to see oneself in the intolerably difficult moment of sorrow, abandoned by God. He, the single, only-begotten Son of God. Oh, what a great mystery! A mystery beyond human comprehension! But beyond the comprehension of the human mind, is the wonderful power of God. And lo, it is through this unfathomable mystery of redemption, that we learn that God is mighty, eternal, and boundless Love. God's love exists. That love moved His Son to set out on the path to suffering and death. It was that love that caused the Father to leave the Son during the moment of His unbearably difficult passion. Divine Love did all of this so that all of the suffering and persecuted, and all of the repentant sinners might be drawn to Him. Oh, Lord, my Saviour! What comfort dost Thou pour into my amazed heart. With Thy passion and death … I profoundly sense that in all my sufferings, I am not alone. Thou, O Lord, art with me. And walking with Thee, I will not fear evil even in the shadow of death….

This homily, pronounced at the epitaphion in the middle of the church, brought many to tears. The nanny of one of the Grand Duchesses was taken away to another room, and only with great difficulty could be calmed down. The homily deeply touched the former Tsar, as he advised me following confession.

The time came to confess the Tsar's children. A messenger arrived to announce "It is time to go. They are already waiting." I put on the epitrachelion [stole, part of a priest's vestment], picked up the cross and Gospel, and following the messenger who led the way, ascended to the children's rooms. In the corner of each Grand Duchess's room was a real iconostasis, filled with a multitude of icons of various sizes, bearing the images of especially venerated saints. Before the iconostasis was a folding analogion covered with a towel, on which were prayer books, service books, and the holy Gospel and a cross. In furniture and decor, the rooms presented an image of a pure and innocent childhood that did not know secular filth. For the prayers before confession, all four of the children gathered in the room in which lay the ill Olga Nikolaevna. Alexei Nikolaevich, dressed in a blue robe with an embroidered decorative braid edging, sat in an armchair. Maria Nikolaevna lay semirecumbent in a large wheelchair, which Anastasia Nikolaevna easily moved about. After the reading of the prayers and a short sermon before confession, Olga Nikolaevna remained in the room. The Heir went off by himself, and Anastasia Nikolaevna wheeled Maria Nikolaevna away. Then I went to the other rooms to confess the others: Alexei, Maria, and Anastasia N[ikolaevny]. I will not relate how the confessions went. My impression was the following: Grant, O Lord, that all children be on as high a moral level as were the children of the former Tsar. Such was their lack of hatred, their humility, their submission to the will of their parents, unquestioning dedication to the will of God, purity of thought and complete ignorance of secular filth—both passionate and sinful—that I was astounded, and could not decide whether I, as a spiritual father, should remind them of sins perhaps unknown to them, and how I should incline them to repent of sins of which they were not aware. Confession of all four lasted one hour and twenty minutes.

At 7:30 p.m. Saturday matins began. During matins, I read the so-called lamentations at the epitaphion, and a procession of the Cross was performed. In the procession, the epitaphion was taken into the altar and around the altar table, entering through the north door and exiting through the south door, then moving through all of the rooms near the Semi-Circular Hall, and returning to the church, first going to the royal doors, and then returning to the center of the church. The epitaphion was carried by Count Benckendorff and by Drs Botkin and Derevenko, who were followed by Nicholas Alexandrovich, Alexandra Feodorovna, Tatiana Nikolaevna, and Anastasia Nikolaevna, and their retinue and servants, all bearing lighted candles. Matins ended at 8:00 p.m., and confession of the ladies of the retinue began: Naryshkina, Dolgorukova, Gendrikova, and Buxhoeveden.

A messenger arrived and announced that Their Majesties would await confession in their bedroom at 10:00 p.m. From 9:00 to 9:30, I sat in my room. The time went by quickly. At 9:40, I went to the church, prayed before the holy altar table, venerated the epitaphion, put on my epitrachelion, took the cross and Gospel and following the messenger, went to Their Majesties' apartments. There, a female servant escorted me through the living rooms to the bedroom, where there stood a single, wide bed. The servant indicated a small room in the corner, a chapel in which the confession of Their Majesties was to take place. No more than two minutes later, the former Sovereign, his spouse, and Tatiana Nikolaevna entered. The Sovereign greeted me, presented the Empress, and indicating his daughter, stated, "This is our daughter Tatiana. You, Batiushka [affectionate term for priest], begin reading the prayers before confession, and we will all pray together." The room/chapel is very small, and is covered from top to bottom with icons, with oil lamps burning before the icons. In a recess in the corner, there stands a special iconostasis, with carved columns and places for famous icons. Before it is a folding analogion, bearing a large ancient altar Gospel, a cross, and many Divine Service books. I did not know where to put the cross and Gospel that I had brought, and so I put them on top of the existing books.

After the reading of the prayers, the Sovereign and his spouse departed, and Tatiana Nikolaevna confessed. She was followed by the Empress, who was clearly agitated, and who apparently had fervently prayed and had decided to confess before the holy cross and Gospel all of the ills of her heart, according to the Orthodox rite, fully cognizant of the greatness of the Mystery.

Then the Sovereign came to confession. Oh, how inexpressibly fortunate I felt to have been made worthy through the mercies of God to become the intermediary between the Heavenly King and the earthly one. For next to me stood the one who was loftier than anyone else living on earth. He was even now the Anointed One given to us by God, one who for twenty-three years, by the law of royal succession, was our reigning Russian Orthodox Tsar. And now, the humble servant of God Nicholas, as a meek lamb, wishing good for all of his enemies, not harboring any offense, praying fervently for Russia's prosperity, deeply believing in her glorious future, on bended knees, gazes upon the cross and the Gospel, and in the presence of my unworthiness, relates to his Heavenly Father the hidden secrets of his long-suffering life, and, reduced to dust before the greatness of the Heavenly King, tearfully asks forgiveness for his transgressions, voluntary and involuntary.

After the reading of the prayer of absolution, and after the kissing of the cross and the Gospel, what joy could I, through my clumsy words of comfort and calm, instill in the heart of one who was cruelly isolated from his people, who until now had been certain of the rightness of his actions as directed to the good of his beloved homeland? When I said, "Oh, Your Majesty, what good you would have done for Russia had you but given her a full constitution, and thereby fulfilled the wishes of the people. For everyone welcomed you as an angel of good, love, and peace." To this, he replied with surprise:

> Can this possibly be true? Yes, everyone betrayed me. I was told that in Petrograd there was anarchy and rebellion, and I decided to go not to Petrograd but to Tsarskoye Selo, and from the Nikolaevskaya Road to turn to Pskov, but the road was already cut off. I decided to return to the front, but the way there was also cut off … And so, alone, without close advisors, deprived of freedom, like a captured criminal, I signed the decree of abdication of the throne, both for myself, and on behalf of my son. I decided that if this was needed for the good of the homeland, I was prepared for anything. I feel sorry for my family!

A tear fell from the eyes of the involuntary sufferer. Then we had a general conversation. Alexandra Feodorovna asked about the health of Fr Alexander. I answered that despite his desire to serve and to be at Tsarskoye Selo, he was as yet unable to do so, as he was still suffering a nervous breakdown. Her Majesty replied, "It is a great pity. Please relay to him our regards and wishes for his good health, for you are his close relative." The Sovereign expressed the same wish for good health, asking about the health of Fr Vasiliev, and adding, "We all love him so fervently. I can explain that his nervous breakdown was brought about in part by the death of his son, whom we all knew, and whose death we all also mourned. Please give him my regards." Nicholas Alexandrovich asked me, "You are now serving in the Feodorovsky Cathedral and no longer in St Catherine's Cathedral? I was very happy to hear that you had consented to serve here with us at the Feodorovsky Cathedral. What is the state of this wonderful cathedral right now?" I replied that all of the buildings of the Feodorovsky Village, together with its cathedral, are temporarily under the jurisdiction of Commissar Golovin. The conversation continued for several minutes on the subject of family life. In the course of conversation, the Empress stated, "I was misunderstood. I wanted good."

April 1, 1917 ~ Saturday has arrived. This is the saint's day of my late wife... I have become despondent in my solitude. I arose at 6:00 a.m., fervently prayed, and at 8:00 went downstairs, and into the altar. At 9:00, the Sovereign said, "We will come to the liturgy, but will read the rule before Communion ourselves." At 8:30, the protodeacon, chanter, and choir members appeared. It was time to begin the service, and there were as yet no prosphora [bread for preparation of the Communion Host]. I begin to worry. Only ten minutes to go, and I cannot begin the proskomedia [rite of preparation of the Host]. What a temptation! I read the hours, went out of the altar, approached Naryshkina and said that I was at a loss as to what to do. But, thanks be to God, at 8:55, the prosphora appeared. I had barely begun the proskomedia, when promptly at 9:00, the Sovereign, his wife, and two daughters, Tatiana and Anastasia, took their appointed places. The liturgy began with vespers, during which I performed the proskomedia. After the Epistle reading, the vestments were changed. All of the black [vestments] were removed and replaced with light ones, announcing the dawn of the coming bright day of the resurrection of Christ. The moment arrived for the communicants to approach the holy chalice. The former Sovereign was first to approach. Giving him the Holy Gifts, I loudly and distinctly stated, "The servant of God the righteous Nicholas Alexandrovich partaketh of the precious and holy Body and Blood of our Lord and God and Saviour Jesus Christ, unto the remission of sins and life everlasting." The same was said for Alexandra Feodorovna. After the liturgy, in full vestments, I went with the holy chalice to commune Olga, Maria, and Alexei, who had already been prepared, and who were waiting in their room upstairs.

Thanks be to God, everything is going well, all are apparently satisfied and relatively calm. At 5:00, a messenger came to my room and extended an invitation from Their Majesties to join them after the Paschal service for a breakfast prepared for eighteen people, and at 1:30 to come receive congratulations on the feast and to exchange the kiss of peace with all of those serving. I was to go first, and after me, all of those serving and living in the palace. Moreover, they ask that on the first day of Pascha, vespers begin at 6:00 p.m., that a moleben be served at 8:30 in the ill children's rooms, and that on Monday, liturgy begin at 11:00 a.m.

Today, on Saturday, dinner consisted of fresh cabbage soup with mushrooms, fried fish, dessert, coffee, a half bottle of white table wine, called "Aidanyl" from their personal cellar, and a bottle of red wine for the protodeacon and chanter. I did not get a chance to rest. At 11:00 p.m., I went to the church to bless the artos and kulichi [Easter breads] and to serve the midnight office, which I did at shortly after 11:00.

Exactly at 11:30 p.m., the Sovereign, his spouse, and two Grand Duchesses, with their retinue, arrived. I rushed to begin matins, opened the royal doors, and went out to distribute candles. Taking his candle, the Sovereign asked whether it was not too early to begin the service, for it was not yet midnight. Then I returned to the altar, and began the proskomedia. At 11:50, I proclaimed "Blessed is Our God," the choir responded with "Amen" and "Thy Resurrection, O Christ our Saviour...." The Procession of the Cross began. At its head, the lantern, then the altar cross, banners, the icon of the resurrection of Christ, the choir members in their purple attire, the clergy in bright Paschal vestments, the Imperial Family, their retinue and all of the servants. Leaving the church hall, we went around the Semi-Circular Hall, and returned to the locked doors of the church, where we stopped. We began the Paschal matins. One could say that the service flew by in the blink of an eye; one-half hour, and it was over. People approached the cross and exchanged the kiss of peace. The Sovereign kissed three times those who approached, with the greeting "Christ is Risen!" Then the liturgy began, and no one left before its completion.

The liturgy lasted exactly one hour, and at 2:00 a.m. the invited guests sat down at the table to break the fast. What an honor! As assigned, I sat down at the first place on the right side, next to the former Empress, while on the left next to me sat Grand Duchess Tatiana Nikolaevna. Opposite us, His Majesty and to either side of him two ladies-in-waiting, Naryshkina and Benckendorff. There were a total of eighteen people at this round table in the library: (1) Her Majesty, (2) the spiritual father, i.e., myself, (3) Tatiana Nikolaevna, (4) Princess Dolgorukova, (5) Schneider, (6) Count Benckendorff, (7) the watch officer, (8) the French instructor, (9) lady-in-waiting Benckendorff, (10) the Sovereign, opposite the Empress, (11) Naryshkina, (12) the palace commandant, (13) a second watch officer, (14) Gendrikova, (15) Buxhoeveden, (16) Derevenko, (17) Botkin, (18) Anastasia Nikolaevna. Along the table wound a braid of live roses.

Onto the table were placed a platter bearing a very large kulich,[23] several plates of hard-boiled eggs dyed red,[24] large roasts of pork and veal on top of which were thinly sliced individual portions, game, various sausages, several cheese pascha, fresh cucumbers, ordinary mustard, and absolutely black salt. The servants served the food in the following order: one took a platter and went to the Sovereign, then to me, and then in order to those to the right of the Empress. Another went to the Empress, then to Naryshkina, and in order to those to the right of the Sovereign. Everything, of course was of the highest quality, perfectly prepared and very tasty; the cheese pascha especially good. I took some of everything—kulich, eggs, pieces of ham and veal, a cucumber, and a cup of coffee with cream. The Empress ate nothing. I said to her "Your Majesty, do you always behave so poorly at the table? You are setting us a bad example." She replied, "I am always on a diet; I will drink a cup of coffee, and that will suffice for me." Wine was also served, but hardly anyone drank any, and although there were goblets filled with champagne, no toasts were proposed; and in general, everything was quite subdued. Conversations were hushed. The Sovereign with a row of ladies, and the Empress with me and with Benckendorff. By the way, in conversation I asked Grand Duchess Tatiana Nikolaevna, about the current functioning of the Tatiana Committee [for assistance to refugees], and why she was not at Ratush, where the anniversary of the founding of the committee and her saint's day were celebrated with such pomp. "But I did not know a thing about that, and in fact I know almost nothing about the matter." Then I asked, "And is there anywhere you would like to go right now, even if only to take a ride somewhere in town or out of town?" "Yes, I would like to, but what can one do; they don't let us go anywhere."

Breakfast lasted no more than half an hour. The Empress rose first. Then everyone else stood up, and made the sign of the cross, which, by the way, they had also done upon sitting down. Then everyone went into the next room and bid one another farewell. The French [tutor] turned out to be a pleasant person. He also asked about Fr Alexander's health, and said that he had recently noted that Fr Alexander did not look well. In general, all of those who served at the palace are well disposed to the spiritual father, and express their sympathy and wish him good health. One more day, and I, God willing, will see my dear children and will share Christian joy together with them on the glorious days of Christ's resurrection. I went to bed toward four o'clock, but was too excited to fall asleep. I was up at 6:00. For a long time I splashed cold water on my head, dressed, and began quietly singing the Paschal canon to myself. At 9:30, I was brought tea and coffee, as well as butter, kulichi, and rolls. I drank a cup of tea and delicious coffee with cream which, although not heavy cream, was excellent. Then I prepared to go to greet people [with the feast].

The official reception began at exactly 11:30. The ceremony dictated that the first to approach was Their Majesties' spiritual father, then the clergy of the palace church and the palace choristers, then all who served and lived at the palace. Count Benckendorff directed the proceedings. The Sovereign stood to receive congratulations, and exchanged the kiss of peace with everyone. He kissed my hand, and I kissed his hand. The Empress stood apart, and to everyone who approached she gave a porcelain egg. I received a very expensive one, bearing a delicate depiction of the crucified Lord. The children of the Sovereign bowed to everyone. One had to go through another set of doors so as not to get in the way of the next person to approach. With this, the entire ceremony concluded.

At 1:00 p.m., lunch was served: a cheese pie, fried chicken, apples in a sweet sauce, coffee, and two bottles of wine, red and white. During lunch, a messenger arrived to announce Her Majesty's request that Paschal vespers be served not in church, but for the sake of the sick children, in the children's room, where a table, icons, and everything necessary would be placed, and her request that it be not at 5:00 p.m. but at 7:00 p.m. I stated, "Relay to Her Majesty, that we and the choir will be there at 7:00 and will fulfill Her Majesty's request." This we did. At 6:30, in full vestments, and accompanied by the choir, we went from the church into a fairly large room filled with a variety of games and toys, tables large and small, various things to amuse children—balalaikas, tambourines, horns, doll houses, and so on. But the main thing, as in all of the children's rooms, was a separate raised area for prayer, where there stood an iconostasis with icons, and before which stood an analogion with religious books and service books. Here we prepared to serve vespers. The former Tsar's entire family, together with their retinue gathered together. The door to the adjacent room, where the sick children lay, was opened. Vespers lasted no more than half an hour. Upon completing vespers, and at the request of Her Majesty, I went to the sick, and offered them the cross to venerate. A special prayer for their health was read. At 8:00, dinner was served: fresh cabbage soup, roast beef with fresh peas, whipped cream with sponge cake, wine, and coffee. At 9:00, I sit alone in my room and read engineer [N. A.] Rynin's book *Air War*, a book I had taken from the table in the library.

April 3, 1917 ~ I got up at 6:00 a.m., sang the Paschal canon, read the rule, and went to the library to return the book, and stayed there to look through the albums lying on the table. At 11:00, the liturgy, attended by the same people who had attended yesterday, began. After the prayer beyond the ambo,[25] I said a few words regarding the feast. At 1:00, lunch was served. And so, our assignment is at an end. The day of our liberation and departure from the palace has arrived. There is nothing to do until Saturday, since, beginning with Tuesday, there are to be no more services.

We wait for the commandant, but he does not come. We receive word that we will not be released from the palace because a decree has been issued banning any communication between those living in the palace and others living at liberty. We did not know what to do, and there was no one to ask. Finally, we were advised that Minister Kerensky, on whom our liberation depended, was not in Petrograd, and that without him the palace commandant could do nothing for us. Thus, the bright days of Christ's joyous resurrection became for us, condemned to isolation, days of sadness and despair. I sit alone in my room, and in my thoughts am transported to my own home, to my loving, sweet family gathered there—to my children, who like baby birds have fled for the cover of their mother's wing, only to find neither mother nor father. But how merciful is the Lord … O Joy! I am summoned to the gates; a meeting has been approved. I put on my riassa [outer cassock] and hurry to be on time. I pass through a series of corridors on the upper level, descend along a long, dirty staircase into the basement. I go through dark and dirty basement passageways. Making my way past coarse soldiers— seated, lying down, standing, moving—who barely make way for me, I enter the so-called reception room—a dingy, fetid, filthy, and crowded room, noisy with the conversations of soldiers seated there as well. But none of that mattered to me, for I saw my sweet children, my dear sweet Manetchka and my dear, beloved Ninotchka. They had found the way, had not been frightened off by the guards, had made me happy, and had made it a festive day. At 8:00 p.m., I had dinner. They served borscht with cheesecake, braised beef with potatoes, ice cream, coffee, and wine. After dinner, I began to read the book *The Truth of Orthodoxy*, sent to me by His Majesty after he had asked me "Do you have anything to read?" and told me that he had a few things.

April 4, 1917 ~ I got up at 6:00 a.m. At 9:00, I was brought tea. I read *The Truth of Orthodoxy* until 11:00, and then went to the Semi-Circular Hall, through the windows of which I could see the Sovereign walking in the garden with his son, accompanied by a convoy of two rifle-bearing soldiers and an officer following behind. The weather was festive— warm and sunny. The Sovereign, returning from his walk, approached me and said in greeting, "What excellent weather today!" Toward 1:00 p.m., I went to my room. Lunch was served at 1:00, and at 3:00 I was again summoned to the reception room, where I was visited by Olga Andreevna. At 4:00, I was again summoned. My children had come and despite the fact that we were in the same oppressive reception room, and in the presence of officers and soldiers, we spent an enjoyable time until 5:00, i.e., a whole hour. The reception room was so unattractive, that as soon as my young granddaughter Galotchka had happily embraced me, she began to beg to go home. At 8:00, the usual dinner and total isolation in my prison. Until 1:00 a.m., I lay on the little couch, reading a book.

April 5, 1917 ~ At 10:00 a.m., I received word that we would not be released from the palace today. I spent a very boring day. Security was augmented, all meetings have ceased, exchange of correspondence, even that which has been opened, is forbidden. Thus, the protodeacon was not allowed to see his wife, and they refused to pass on a letter that had already been opened and read by the watch officer.

April 6, 1917 ~ I got up as usual at 6:00 a.m. Sang the Paschal canon and the entire resurrection service to myself. At 9:00, I had a cup of tea with cream and rolls, and sat down to read Poselyanin's book *At Prayer in Calm and in the Storm*, sent to me by the lady-in-waiting Hendrikova. About noon, I saw through my window that the Sovereign was taking a walk along the garden path with his son and an augmented detachment of guards. At 4:00, I walked out onto the balcony, while the Sovereign and his son were walking in the park not far from the balcony. Returning to the room, he said hello and asked me, "So you are still here? They have not released you?" At 9:00 p.m., the palace commandant came by to see me, and gave me small consolation by telling me that we would soon be released. Until late at night, I read the papers and Goncharov's novel *Oblomov*.

April 7, 1917 ~ Got up at 6:00, sang the Paschal canon, drank a cup of tea, and looking out the sole window of my room, admired the gardeners' work in the Tsar's garden, freeing the bushes from the ropes restraining them, and how, those bushes, liberated, joyously stretched out their branches and assumed their former shape. Oh, that we might soon be liberated as well! At 4:00 p.m., I wandered along the balcony, and watched the Sovereign, his son, and others cutting ice from the ditch and dragging it onto the field. In the evening, I read, and went to bed at 1:00 a.m.

April 8, 1917 ~ The same as yesterday. Solitude. One becomes used to anything. Today at 6:30 p.m., I served the all-night vigil. Everyone but the ill Grand Duchesses Olga and Maria attended. After the service, had dinner, and in the evening read the rule and prepared for tomorrow's Divine Liturgy.

April 9, 1917 ~ Sunday. I began to serve the liturgy at 11:00 a.m. Somehow prayed especially fervently. Gave a homily on the words of the Gospel "and He showed them His hands and His feet and His side…" I had taken the ideas from the wonderful homilies of Dmitry of Rostov. All listened very attentively. At 1:00, I had lunch and went to watch the Imperial Family, with sweat on their brows, entertain themselves by pulling ice from the ditch. From five o'clock on, I sat in my room and read *Oblomov*. How appropriate…

April 10, 1917 ~ I addressed a statement to Kerensky regarding my release from the Alexander Palace.

> To Minister Alexander Feodorovich Kerensky from the rector of the Feodorovsky Cathedral. As rector of the Feodorovsky Cathedral, as the dean of the military churches of Tsarskoye Selo and Pavlovsk, as director of the Diocesan District Educational Committee, as representative of the Tatiana Committee for assistance to refugees, as teacher of religion in the schools and orphanages, I humbly request the Minister to release me from the need for continued presence at the Alexander Palace, and thereby to afford me the opportunity to carry out the responsibilities of my vocation, which cannot be put off. I was summoned to the palace to serve in the palace church during Passion Week and during the first two days of Pascha, and I have fulfilled those duties to the letter. As to serving in the palace church on Sundays and Feast Days in the future, I hereby obligate myself to appear at the appointed days and times, on the condition that I have authorization, and am granted both entry

and unimpeded exit following completion of the services. At the same time, I must advise you that in my absence from my post, refugees will not receive their monetary allowances, teachers in parish schools may be left without salaries, the schools without their examinations, and the parish in military churches without direction. I have been torn from my work, home, and family, and personally find myself in extremely uncertain circumstances as to means of support. I have yet to receive from the military my earned salary.

At 11:00 a.m., the liturgy began. The same people came to pray. After lunch, I walked about the garden near the balcony of the Semi-Circular Hall, and took a few steps down the path, when the sentry standing at his post gruffly announced, "It is forbidden to leave the balcony." I dared to reply, "I am not under arrest, and may freely walk along the paths in the little garden which is surrounded by the guards." Moving twenty steps away from the balcony, I sat down on a bench and sat there for ten minutes. Another time I heard the prohibition from him in a softer tone, "Pops, pops, where are you going—it's forbidden!" From 5:00 p.m. on, I was in my room reading books sent to me by Gendrikova and the *Evening Times* newspapers.

April 11, 1917 ~ There is no service. We awaited Kerensky, who was promised to come to the Palace to inspect the guards. But Kerensky did not come. At 2:00 p.m., Benckendorff came to relay Her Majesty's direction that I was to serve the Divine Liturgy on Wednesday the twelfth at 11:00 a.m., and that today, Tuesday, I was to serve the vigil at 6:30 p.m. in the former Heir's bedroom, where all of the children and servants would be assembled.

All day I sat in my room, and through the window watched the former Sovereign and others walking in the garden. The former Heir was taken past my window in a wheelchair. Grand Duchess Anastasia Nikolaevna saw me in the window and loudly said to her mother, "Over there, the batiushka is looking [at us]." She smiled, looked up, and nodded to me. At 6:30, I served the vigil in the child's room. A door was open to the adjacent room, where lay the ill Grand Duchesses Olga and Maria, and the Heir, who had caught a cold while pulling ice from the ditch.

April 12, 1917 ~ Wednesday. All of the same people attended and prayed at Divine Liturgy served at the appointed time. We await Kerensky and are afraid to miss him. He is to be at the palace at 2:00 p.m. Everything has taken on an air of expectation. There is unusual activity in all of the halls. Servants are seen more often throughout the palace, duty officers walk by, even the soldiers on guard duty stand at their posts and behave themselves more appropriately. The choir members, protodeacon, chanter, and I take turns on watch, and hold discussions with the servants; even the former Sovereign, before going for his usual walk in his garden, directed that he immediately be informed of the minister's arrival. We wait one hour, two, three, four; still he has not come. Finally, at the fifth hour, word comes, "He has arrived." Immediately, without stopping, he walked into His Majesty's room. We all crowded together in the corridor near the door to the Sovereign's room. I handed my statement to the palace commandant. I did not get to see the minister, but from the commandant who had been in the Sovereign's room and had spoken about us to the minister, we received the joyous news of our release. And so, today, on Wednesday, April 12, at 8:00 p.m., we are free. We did not want to dine, we gathered up our belongings: books, laundry, etc., and sent them to the guard room for inspection. When everything was ready, we ourselves appeared at the guard room, where we were searched and received permission to leave the palace. A carriage was provided. We transferred our bundles and traveling bags, and I, signing myself with the sign of the cross, set off for home. I was home by 4:00.

April 15, 1917 ~ At 6:00 p.m., a horse was provided to take me to the palace to serve the vigil. I had gone under the condition that I spend the night in the palace, but as every arrival and departure was accompanied by a search in the filthy guard room, after long discussions with some unidentified persons, the palace commandant ordered that we be released under guard from the palace, and returned at 10:00 a.m. to serve the liturgy. The evening service took place in the usual manner.

April 16, 1917 ~ Served the liturgy, gave a homily on the heav[enly] myrrh-bearers. The same people were in attendance.

April 22 and 23, 1917 ~ The saint's day of the former Tsarina Alexandra Feodorovna. It had already been announced on the sixteenth that Her Majesty wishes me to bring the akathist [to the Great Martyr St George] to be read at the all-night vigil on the twenty-second. This was done. At 6:30 p.m., the vigil service began. The entire Imperial Family came, dressed in bright, festive garments. The son, four daughters, and their parents, and the entire staff of servants. After the six psalms and the small litany, the akathist to the Great Martyr St George was read. At the end, there was a special prayer for Her Majesty Tsarina Alexandra. The next day, all of the same people, dressed in festal garments, came to the Divine Liturgy. Before the liturgy, we served a moleben for health, and during the liturgy, instead of the usual prayer for victory, a special prayer to the Holy Martyr Empress Alexandra was read. The liturgy concluded with my sermon on the occasion of the feast. As they approached the cross, I congratulated the Sovereign and the Empress, giving them each a prosphora [blessed bread]. To the Empress, I extended my congratulations on her saint's day, and wished her spiritual peace, health, patience to endure those difficult days, and help from the Lord, according to the prayers of the Holy Martyr Alexandra. In response, the Empress expressed her thanks, making an effort to smile, but her smile was that of one who was suffering and ill. Everyone in the church, upon kissing the cross, made a silent bow toward the place where, near the screen, set apart from everyone else, the Imperial Family stood. That was all to distinguish this day from any ordinary weekday spent in strict confinement. It saddened me to the point of tears.

At mid-Pentecost, on April 26, there was no service.

April 29, 1917 ~ Saturday. The usual vigil, with the usual faithful, except for the former Heir. The same sorrow and the same solitude. Joy and comfort in prayer...

April 30, 1917 ~ I served the liturgy, and gave a homily on the words of the Gospel "God *is* Spirit, and those who worship Him must worship in spirit and truth..."[26] I was speaking about enduring spiritual suffering, which faces man, abandoned by everyone, in an inexpressible, oppressive state, horrifies him, and the sole comfort he finds is in prayer. At this point there escaped from someone such an irrepressible, loud and powerful, heartrending sigh, that it amazed all of the listeners. And that response of spiritual torment emanated from the place where only the Imperial Family was standing. After the service, everyone venerated the cross.

May 5, 1917 ~ I served the vigil, and on May 6, the Divine Liturgy. Before the liturgy, there was a moleben at 10:00. The entire Imperial Family came to the liturgy and prayed fervently, celebrating the Sovereign's birthday. It was announced that there was no more liturgical wine, and I asked to be furnished with ordinary red table wine. I was brought half a bottle of some type of wine, which was used for the service. In the evening, I served the usual vigil, and on Sunday, May 7, the Divine Liturgy. The same people came to pray, and the ordinary homily was given. In general, after each liturgy, I give a little sermon.

May 10, 1917 ~ Ascension. At 6:30 p.m., the festal vigil with the bringing of the [festal] icon to the center of the church, the litya [breaking of the bread], and blessing of the loaves.

May 11, 1917 ~ Divine Liturgy at 11:00. Thanks be to God, the entire Imperial Family has recovered, and attends all of the services and attentively listens to the sermons; this is apparent from the fact that as soon as I begin the sermon, they all move forward a little, and stand there until the end. After the service, as I went through the nave, I greeted everyone, congratulated them on the feast, and spoke to Dr Botkin and the French [tutor], about Fr Alexander's state of health, as they were most interested in it.

May 13 and 14, 1917 ~ Saturday and Sunday. The usual service at its appointed time. The entire Imperial Family, seven persons, stands and prays from the beginning to the end of the service. Naryshkina was not among the ladies of the retinue. I learned that she had been unable to endure her imprisonment, had become ill, and was carried out of the palace and transferred to an apartment in the Catherine Palace. The entire Imperial Family had gone to her room to bid her farewell and see her off. Thus, the number of people close to the Tsar's family was diminished by one. On May 14, Naryshkina sent a maid to ask me to visit her, which I did. I visited her on both May 16 and 17, and according to her wishes, prayed for her health, heard her confession, and gave her Holy Communion. She was very happy, prayed with tears in her eyes, and, by the way, told me that my sermons served as a great comfort to the Imperial Family, suffering in bondage.

May 20, 1917 ~ Saturday before Trinity Sunday. The vigil was more festive [than usual]. The icon, decorated with live flowers, was brought out into the center of the church. The polyeleos and blessing of the loaves took place. Beginning with today, whole loaves of bread, even prosphora, will be given only to the former Sovereign and the former Empress. And their children will receive only small pieces. There is no more flour! All seven were at the divine services, and as far as I could see, were more calm. The Grand Duchesses even exchanged glances and with childish smiles looked at the watch officers and soldiers who approached to venerate the icon, and then did not bow in the direction of the Imperial Family, the custom observed by others after they venerate the icon and receive the priest's blessing.

May 21, 1917 ~ The liturgy began at 10:30 a.m. The entire Imperial Family was in bright festal attire, the former Sovereign and his son wore ordinary khaki military blouses with the cross of the Order of St George on their chests. Twenty-five bouquets of live roses and other flowers were brought into the altar for distribution to those in attendance during the Pentecost vespers. The chanter distributed the bouquets after the liturgy. At vespers, I read the prayers in full and on bended knees, and everyone prayed fervently. The entire service lasted one hour and forty-five minutes.

After the service, Dr Botkin and the French tutor were waiting for me next door. Botkin asked me a perplexing question, requesting that I explain why several books from the Old Testament were missing from the latest edition of the Bible. I explained that there were twenty-three books in the canon of the Old Testament, and that other instructive texts could be included only as instructive, and not as canonical books, i.e., not as books belonging to the Old Testament. The French tutor asked about the state of health of Fr Alexander, whom he greatly respected, and about General Petrov, who was responsible for educating and raising the

Tsar's children. Passing through other palace rooms, I saw the former Empress off in the distance, standing and apparently waiting next to an old elevator. As I reached her, I paused, made the usual bow, and she, extending her hand to me, said with a smile, "Congratulations on the Feast." I kissed her hand and wished her good health. It was impossible to say more, for next to us stood an officer and a soldier, and also a hall-porter and a sentry. The former Tsar's family and the Tsar himself tirelessly work the soil. In their garden, they have tilled sixty separate beds, which they have planted with a variety of garden vegetables, as well as potatoes. They set an example for any peasant worker, who now received twelve rubles per day for tilling garden soil.

May 22, 1917 ~ The Day of the Holy Spirit. Liturgy was, as usual, at 11:00 a.m. We did not serve matins. Only the Sovereign and two Grand Duchess, Olga and Tatiana Nikolaevna attended. They asked that I come to serve a vigil on Wednesday and liturgy on Thursday. Today I met with the palace commandant, who asked about my health and work, and whether my family and spiritual children had calmed down after seeing me at liberty. I got word by telephone from the palace that horses would be sent to me at 5:30 p.m., but they had not yet arrived by 6:00. Despite the rain and mud, I went on foot, and a good thing, too, for the horses were not dispatched even after 6:00.

May 24, 1917 ~ The entire Imperial Family and the already very diminished number of remaining retainers attended the vigil. Loaves were not blessed for the simple reason that they could not be obtained. They told us that soon because of the shortage of flour we would no longer have prosphora either. Buxhoeveden asked for prayers for the health of her sick mother, Ludmilla. I relayed to Botkin that Petrov had undergone a successful laparotomy, that no cancer had been found, and that although he was weak, his prognosis was not hopeless.

May 25, 1917 ~ The former Empress' birthday. Served a moleben before the liturgy, while only the servants were in church. The entire Imperial Family came to the liturgy at 11:00 a.m., and as usual I gave a homily. There were no congratulations or ceremonies, not even an invitation to drink a cup of tea. Utter desolation. I was also asked to come to the palace today and serve a panikhida [requiem] service for Ludmilla Buxhoeveden, who had reposed in Kazan. On leaving the palace, I admonished the gate guards, and told the duty officer about their inappropriate behavior. It is not enough that the soldiers on guard stand in an unseemly manner, but they also curse loudly, using the most awful and unprintable words. The officer would only say, "Comrades! You should be ashamed of yourselves!" And the comrades remained comrades… At 6:00 p.m., together with the protodeacon and choir, I served the panikhida. The daughter of the deceased, as well as the Empress and her daughters, were in attendance.

May 27, 1917 ~ Saturday. At 6:00 p.m., the second panikhida for the handmaiden of God Ludmilla Buxhoeveden was served, and was followed at 6:30 by the usual Sunday vigil. I entered the palace by way of the kitchen gate and along the lower corridor, without even an escort, straight to the church, where lady-in-waiting Buxhoeveden was waiting for me. She asked that tomorrow I hear her confession before the liturgy and then commune her after the liturgy. After vigil, I got word by telephone that Dr Botkin's mother-in-law was extremely ill and requested that I come to her tomorrow with the Holy Gifts. I did so, and communed the ill Elena. Botkin himself was caring for her, and had been released from the palace for that specific purpose. I learned that the Tsar's children were now being educated—especially in English—by their parents, assisted by two ladies-in-waiting. Today I had a run-in with soldiers who were lying on the grass near the Feodorovsky Cathedral. A soldier was brazen enough to make a speech about the filth-eating "popes" [priests], concluding with the words, "So, you are on your way to wag your tongue in the church. That's all you all do, is babble." Nonetheless, the soldiers conceded that one should not trample the grass without cause, and that my criticism was justified. They got up and left.

May 28, 1917 ~ Sunday. I was allowed into the palace by way of the rear entrance. I went to the church at 10:00 a.m. and confessed Buxhoeveden. By the way, I asked the guard to go into the next room, and he did so. At 11:00, the liturgy began. Only Alexei Nikolaevich was absent. The

Empress relayed an inquiry through her valet about Fr Alexander's health, and wanted to know his apartment number. She also asked that I come tomorrow at 11:00 a.m. to serve a Thanksgiving moleben on the occasion of Tatiana Nikolaevna's birthday. At the conclusion of the liturgy, after everyone had left the church, I communed Sophie Buxhoeveden, who had asked me to do so. Everyone left, but the Empress remained in the church and was present during the Communion. It seemed to me that the Sovereign had a very pale, suffering appearance, and was very ill. Something is bothering him, and he is silently, patiently, enduring his suffering. He prays fervently, often on his knees.

May 29, 1917 ~ Monday. For one-half hour we have been waiting at the palace gate for permission to enter. The curious, the comrades, and idle folk begin to gather. The duty officer came out onto the driveway, and sent someone to tell us that we should go to the kitchen gates. We went, and again had to wait. Finally, we were permitted to go, under military escort, along the filthy corridor to the church. We were fifteen minutes late. By the time we entered the nave, the entire retinue had already assembled. As soon as I appeared, so did the Imperial Family. The moleben lasted twenty minutes. We commemorated the righteous servants of God Nicholas Alexandrovich, his spouse Alexandra Feodorovna, and their children: Alexei Nikolaevich, Olga Nikolaevna, Tatiana Nikolaevna, Maria Nikolaevna, and Anastasia Nikolaevna. There was no singing of "Many years." The children, smiling and appearing satisfied, approached the cross. I was quickly released from the palace.

June 3 and 4, 1917 ~ Saturday and Sunday. I did not receive the usual invitation to serve in the palace church, but horses were provided at 6:00 p.m. I was home; I dressed, and went. Vigil began at 6:30 p.m. The entire Imperial Family and their servants attended the service, which as usual lasted one hour. After the service I went home on foot, for they had erroneously told the driver to come at 8:00 p.m. On Sunday, the liturgy began at the usual hour, and continued from 11:00 to noon. The Sovereign, the Empress, and all five children attended. I gave a homily on the Gospel reading regarding the first chosen disciples of Christ. I touched on the people's election of Most-Reverend Benjamin to the cathedra of the Petrograd Diocese; despite the fact that the Most-Reverend Benjamin did not yet have his own diocese, and was only a vicar bishop and the youngest of the candidates, he was elected by a very large majority. I was asked to serve a moleben tomorrow.

June 5, 1917 ~ Monday. At noon, I served a moleben at the palace church on the occasion of Anastasia Nikolaevna's birthday. She had just turned sixteen. The entire Imperial Family and their retainers prayed at the moleben. Before offering the cross to be kissed, I said a few words about the joy parents experience in having children who manifest a high moral standard, sincere love, childlike faith, and wholehearted obedience, and what joy children feel living under the vigilant and comfortable protection of their mother and father. As he venerated the cross, the Sovereign said, "Thank you, batiushka, for your kind and comforting words." The moleben lasted one-half hour. A prayer on bended knees was read, commemorating by name all of the members of the Royal Family: the servants of God Nicholas Alexandrovich, his spouse Alexandra Feodorovna, and their children: Alexei Nikolaevich, Olga Nikolaevna, Tatiana Nikolaevna, Maria Nikolaevna, and Anastasia Nikolaevna. I was invited to come to the palace on Saturday, June 10, to serve the vigil.

June 10, 1917 ~ Saturday 6:00 p.m. I drove up to the palace gate in a carriage, and asked the sentry to call the duty officer to permit me to enter the palace. Five minutes later, the officer appeared with two soldiers and demanded my pass. I told him that for the past three months, I had been allowed to enter without a pass. The young officer said, "It is forbidden. I do not know you, and who can vouch for you?" "All right," I said, "if you do not allow me in, I will go home. Tell that to the commandant." Then the comrade reconsidered, and telephoned the palace adjutant. The gates were opened and I was allowed to pass. At this point, Protodeacon, the chanter, and the four choristers arrived. And so it went each time, and at the same place! The entire Imperial Family, all seven members, prayed at the vigil. The service lasted exactly one hour. We were allowed to leave the palace without incident.

June 11, 1917 ~ Sunday. The liturgy, served as usual, was attended by the entire Imperial Family and those serving in the palace, with the exception of Naryshkina and Botkin, who were away from the palace by reason of illness. Upon completion of the liturgy at noon, I went to St Catherine's Cathedral in the city and took part in the serving of a moleben before the miraculous icon of the Holy Hierarch and Wonderworker St Nicholas, which had been brought in solemn procession from Kolpino to Tsarskoye Selo. Wednesday will be Grand Duchess Maria Nikolaevna's birthday, and for that reason I was requested to come serve a moleben at noon.

June 14, 1917 ~ Wednesday, Grand Duchess Maria Nikolaevna's birthday. I served a Thanksgiving moleben at the palace church. Except for the Tsarina, the entire Imperial Family was still walking in their park when we were already standing in our vestments in the church. Going though the hall, all of the children cast smiling glances in our direction and hurried to their rooms in order to change and be on time for the moleben. At exactly 12:00, the moleben started. The former Sovereign, the former Empress, and their five children were present.

Before the kissing of the cross, I said, "On Sunday, June 11, the miraculous icon of the Holy Hierarch and Wonderworker St Nicholas was brought in solemn procession from Kolpino to Tsarskoye Selo, and was placed in St Catherine's Cathedral. After the service in the palace, I managed to go to the cathedral and take part in the general prayers before the icon of St Nicholas, that by the saint's prayers and the mercies of the Lord fruitful rain might descend upon our dry and thirsty land. I prayed ardently and intensely for this honorable house and all those who dwell herein, together with their servants… Yes, in this present awful time, we are particularly in need of the Holy Hierarch's assistance. We need this rule of faith at this uncertain, vacillating, faithless time. We need this image of meekness and Christian love for the wild, arrogant, embittered people who thirst after bloody executions, for the open and secret enemies of our homeland. People who have illegally seized others' property and inheritance, people greedy for acquisition, those who have lost both shame and conscience, and mercenary predators, are in need of absolution. During his life, the Holy Hierarch Nicholas was accessible to all. He was a father to orphans, a nourisher of the poor, comforter to those who mourn and weep, protector of the oppressed, defender of the unjustly condemned, those languishing and suffering in bondage. As the worthy one of God was in life, so is he today. Let us pray to him; may he petition our Lord the Father of the Heavenly Realm to grant us peace, tranquility, health, spiritual calm, and may he restore order to our land, which is perishing from sedition and pillage." Venerating the cross, the Sovereign said, "I thank you." A new order is noticeable. The palace square is clean, the sentries on watch stand in an appropriate manner, and for the first time, I did not have to stand and wait at the gate for the duty officer to allow me to pass.

June 17 and 18, 1917 ~ So far, there is complete order. I did not have to wait for the duty officer. The vigil started in the palace church at its regular time. With the exception of the former Heir, Alexei Nikolaevich, the entire Imperial Family came to pray at the vigil. On Sunday, the entire Imperial Family attended the liturgy and heard my homily on the Gospel regarding humility and meekness as the highest Christian virtues and on the life of the Holy Hierarch Nicholas. There are no [major] feast days, and so I was not asked to return before Saturday at 6:30 p.m.

June 20, 1917 ~ Tuesday. At 9:00 a.m., I received a telephone message that horses would be provided at noon to take me to the palace, where at 12:30 p.m. there was to be a Thanksgiving moleben on the occasion of our armed forces' offensive and military victory on the western front at Koniukha-Byshka. At the appointed time, and in the presence of the entire Royal Family and their retinue, the moleben was served; the protodeacon intoned the prayer wishing "Many years" for the God-preserved Russian Power, for the Christian armed forces, and for all Orthodox Christians. The choir sang "Many years," and "God is with us." I said, "Glory and thanksgiving to our Lord God! Sense has triumphed over madness. It is clear that Our Father in Heaven has heard the tearful and fervent prayers of the faithful. The entire people, tortured by staggeringly awful events, has leapt up in spirit. The Christ-loved armed forces, having signed themselves with the sign of the cross, made a concerted effort and surged at the evil-doing enemy, and breaking through the great enemy defenses, won a glorious victory, causing the enemy to flee, and taking 10,000 enemy soldiers prisoner. May the Lord grant that our victorious effort quickly bring to an end this awful, bloody world war, and bring peace, order, and calm to all peoples."

June 24, 1917 ~ Vigil at the Alexander Palace was served at the usual time and in the usual order. The only difference was that at the veneration of the cross, Their Majesties were followed by their children, in chronological order: Olga, Tatiana, Maria, Anastasia, and finally Alexei. In the past, Alexei Nikolaevich had always followed his parents. By the way, another difference lay in the fact that this time, for my transportation, a single horse, and not a carriage, as had been the case in the past, was furnished. For a long time, they would not release us from the palace, and finally they delayed us at the gates. I asked the soldier who was sent instead of the duty officer to escort us, "Why are you treating us in this way? Forcing us to stand in the rain and cold at the gates and wait for something? We are free people with responsibilities!" He demanded of us some kind of pass from the palace commandant. I replied, "And do you yourselves have such a pass?" The soldier, displeased with that answer, directed the sentry to detain the clergy, and twirling a cigarette with his hands and wetting it with saliva, he went off into the palace, leaving us to stand at the gates. However, at that moment, an order was given to the guard by telephone to allow us to pass, and we were released.

June 25, 1917 ~ Sunday. Divine Liturgy is served at the usual time and attended by the whole Royal Family. I spoke about the Holy Land, and about the holy places, in which St John the Baptist, whose memory was celebrated on June 24, had been born, lived, and preached. On walking through the halls and exchanging a few phrases with others, I noticed an air of heavy oppression among those living in confinement.

June 28, 1917 ~ Wednesday. I was told by telephone that there would be services today and tomorrow, the twenty-ninth. Horses would be provided at 6:00 p.m. Vigil began at 6:30 p.m. It was attended by the entire Imperial Family except for the Sovereign, whom we had seen in a palace corridor upon our arrival. He came out of a room in front of us, and crossed the corridor to the other side, from which one could surmise that he had free access to all of the rooms on the lower floor of the palace. The former Heir followed his sisters, and was the last to venerate the cross.

June 29, 1917 ~ Thursday. Liturgy at 11:00 a.m. The entire Imperial Family was in church. I spoke of the holy apostles Saints Peter and Paul. I developed the theme that one of the apostles burned with love and a boundless devotion to Christ, while the other burned with an equal, if not greater, hatred and anger toward the Son of God, and that neither of these, without the special grace of God, was of any significance in the acceptance and recognition of the Incarnate Truth. The Apostle Peter, after thrice confessing the faith, thrice renounced Christ, while the Apostle Paul could be enlightened only by an extraordinary miracle, worked upon him for his enlightenment. The liturgy ended at noon, and without having lunch, we left the palace.

July 1, 1917 ~ Saturday. The day is one hour shorter, as at night the clock hands are moved forward from 12:00 to 1:00. We had the usual vigil, attended by the entire Imperial Family and all of their servants. Horses were provided to me and to the rest of the clergy with some delay. Entry and exit were without incident, and the palace clocks were reset according to the new orders.

July 2, 1917 ~ Sunday. At 10:00 a.m., prior to the liturgy, I, together with the protodeacon and the choir, served a panikhida for the late Ludmilla Buxhoeveden, on the occasion of the fortieth day following her death. Liturgy began at 11:00 a.m., its appointed time. The Imperial Family and their servants had assembled by the beginning of the liturgy, and the former Heir Alexei Nikolaevich quietly arrived at the cherubic hymn. He came unnoticed because he used a separate entrance, and went straight into the altar to serve as an acolyte. He would take the censer from the chanter, return it to its place, and would hand it as needed to the protodeacon. This was the first time that his parents' beloved child had shown an inclination to personally participate in divine services.

> At the conclusion of the liturgy, I spoke on the words of the Gospel.
> When Jesus saw their faith, He said to the paralytic, "Son, be of good cheer…"[27] The Lord healed the paralytic, according to the faith and prayers offered on behalf of the paralytic, who was too weak to offer prayers and petitions. This is what we should

do, whenever and for whatever reason we find ourselves unable or too weak. When we cannot rely on our own prayers, we should ask for those of others. But of whom? Of those who are closer to God and who are well disposed to us. And who are they? These are the saints of God, these are the people who love us, these are our relatives, and, finally, these are the ones whom God Himself has directed to pray for us. The Apostle James said to call the presbyters of the Church and have them pray. In asking for the prayers of others, we will also strive ourselves to pray for others. How can you sometimes help another person? You want to help, you need to help, you suffer, you mourn, sometimes more than the mourner, and you find no way to help. Only prayer will help, will give life and strength.

July 8, 1917 ~ Saturday. At 6:30 p.m., served the usual vigil, attended by the entire Imperial Family, recently returned from a walk. I saw the children hurrying, and driving the Tsarina in a wheelchair through the palace; the Tsar walked alongside her. Vigil lasted [one half] of an hour, and ended earlier than usual.

July 9, 1917 ~ Sunday. The Divine Liturgy went from 11:00 a.m. to noon. The Imperial Family and an already reduced number of servants. The heir came into the altar, and was given some wine mixed with hot water, and a piece of antidoron [literally, "instead of the Gifts," prosphora given to those who have not received Communion]. I spoke on the Gospel story of the healing of the blind man. Painting a picture of the blind man's impoverished state after he lost his human vision, I turned to the subject of spiritual blindness.

Oh, how many people in the awful time we are enduring have blinded their wisdom. You are involuntarily seized by horror when you see and hear the extent of human blindness. There is no lie that a man blinded by passions will not present as the truth. There is no untruth that he will not begin to justify. There is no crime of which he is incapable. The voice of passion blinds all, not only the voice of reason, but the voice of blood relationship. Brother rises up against brother, son against father, daughter against mother. But worst of all, man—the created—rises up against God, Creator and Planner of the universe. By His great mercy, may God preserve us from such blindness.

I was asked to come on July 11, at noon to serve a moleben. The chanter asked for flowers to be prepared to decorate the icon of St Olga, but he was refused, being told that bringing flowers into the palace was no longer permitted. The flowers from the former royal hothouses are being sold. Even the potted palms have been removed from the palace halls, and been sent to who knows where. There are reductions and cutbacks in all areas.

July 11, 1917 ~ St Olga's Day. At noon, we served a moleben in the palace church, before the icon of Holy R[ighteous] P[rincess] Olga, which had been brought from the rooms of Olga Nikolaevna, who was celebrating her saint's day. The entire Imperial Family and their small retinue assembled five minutes late. The holy icon was decorated simply, with greens and with some plain little roses. Before the veneration of the cross and icon, I said:

> As history teaches us, the H[oly] R[ighteous] G[reat] P[rincess] Olga , whose memory we celebrate today, was by birth from Pskov. It happened that she became the wife of Great Prince Igor of Kiev, and after his death in 962 became regent, ruling the principality of Rus' on behalf of her minor son Sviatoslav. Living as a pagan, [in a milieu] where perfidy, malice, vengeance were considered a legal norm and even heroically praiseworthy, Olga, in a pagan manner, perfidiously and maliciously dispatched the enemies who had murdered her husband, Igor. However, gifted with great intellect and a heart responsive to all good, she soon changed, recognized the purity of the teachings of the Gospel and Christian love, and, upon being baptized, was completely reborn, becoming a person who was pious, humble, and desirous of doing good not only for her friends but for her enemies. This is how great and unimaginably good is the Christian faith, and how fortunate are we all to have been born, baptized, and brought up as Christians. Grant

as well, O Lord, that by the prayers of St Olga, the dear one who celebrates her saint's day, and who has been raised in the Orthodox faith by her righteous parents, may always remain as pure, innocent, humble, and profoundly loving as she has been to this day.

Upon venerating the cross, the Sovereign said, "Thank you." All of the rest silently kissed the cross and the hand which sprinkled them with holy water. By the time we left the altar, there was not a single person in the nave, and the guard had gone ahead, escorting the members of the choir. Each time, the former Heir was the last to approach the cross. I was furnished one horse, which had belonged to D. N. Lohmann, warden of the Feodorovsky Cathedral, and which was now the property of the government.

July 15, 1917 ~ Saturday. The vigil is served at the usual time and the entire Imperial Family, with the same complement of palace servants, attended the divine service. At the close of the service, and on behalf of Her Majesty, the Empress's valet asked about Fr Alexander Vasiliev's health, about where he was living, and whether he was to return home soon. He announced that the Empress would like to have Divine Liturgy served in the palace church on July 19, the day of St Seraphim, with a vigil to be served on the eighteenth. To this, I responded that the Feodorovsky Cathedral celebrates the patronal feast day of its crypt chapel on that date, and festal services were to be served there. As rector of the cathedral, I would like to serve in my own cathedral. However, if Her Majesty wishes that there be a service in the palace, and no replacement can be found, then I will fulfill Her Majesty's wish and will serve at the palace.

July 16, 1917 ~ Sunday. The liturgy was at its usual time, and the entire Imperial Family came to pray. As before, the Heir was the first to approach the cross after his parents did, and was followed by the Grand Duchesses. Protodeacon troubled me by doing the wrong Gospel reading. Instead of reading about the feeding of the 5,000 with five loaves, he read of the driving away of the demons in the country of the Gadarenes, and I had to say something other than what I had planned before the liturgy. I remembered the words "Lord, instill in my unworthy lips words which are worthy of glorifying Thy Holy Name." And the Lord helped me. Sharply delineating the current state of the Russian people, who had misunderstood the gift of freedom and had turned this divine gift into madness, bringing anarchy and degradation, [[I compared it to] the state to which one of the higher spirits, the fallen angel [Lucifer], had brought himself. He had rebelled against his God and Creator, and in his mad self-will had so debased himself that he decided to ask as a favor to be put into a herd of unclean beasts, a herd of swine. I closed with the prayer, "O Lord, have mercy on us, enlighten us, and teach us to do not our own will, but Thy Divine Will." After leaving the church, Count Benckendorff relayed to me the Empress's wish that on July 19 I serve at the Feodorovsky Cathedral, and that there be no service in the palace on that day. She requested that on Saturday, July 22, on Maria Feodorovna's saint's day, I come to the palace and serve a moleben at 6:00 p.m. prior to the vigil.

July 22, 1917 ~ Saturday. At 6:00 p.m., a moleben, attended by the entire Imperial Family, was served to Equal-to-the-Apostles St Mary Magdalene. "Many years" was not sung. Immediately after the moleben, the vigil began; it ended fifteen minutes earlier than usual.

July 23, 1917 ~ Divine Liturgy was served as usual, at its usual time, and attended by the same people. The Heir served in the altar, and toward the end of the liturgy went into the nave, where the entire Imperial Family was standing. With them, he listened to my talk on how the memory of St Seraphim had been celebrated in our Feodorovsky Cathedral. Among other things, I said, "I offer heartfelt thanks for the fact that I was able to serve the festal vigil and Divine Liturgy in the wonderful crypt church of St Seraphim, where there have been preserved so many memories both of beautiful hierarchical services, and of the great people of prayer who, especially during days of fasting and repentance, loved to fervently pray before the reliquary in which were carefully housed both a relic of the body of venerable St Seraphim, but also a piece of his clothing, and a piece of the stone upon which he prayed." Everyone listened attentively, and I sensed that the spirit of St Seraphim was with those who were praying. Descending the steps after the liturgy, I could not help but be struck by the sight of filth, slovenliness, and seediness in this marvelously beautiful, always perfectly clean, royal entranceway. The entire staircase leading to Their Majesties' rooms was soiled with bird droppings, cigarette butts, and garbage that had not been swept away. The palace courtyard and the paths ringing the palace were overgrown with dirty weeds, while the lawns had been trampled by the guards.

July 29, 1917 ~ Saturday. At 6:00 p.m., two horse-drawn carriages, coming from different directions, drove up to the palace at the same time. I got out of one, while my concelebrant, Fr Nicholas, and the chanter got out of the other. After standing at the gates for a short while until the duty officer arrived, we walked into the park, and saw that something unusual was happening. The courtyard has been swept, the garbage removed, the staircase has been cleaned, the sentries seem to be in a better mood, and among the so-called comrades on the porch, there appears to be an especially free and easy air of invigoration. From the duty officer's words, we realized the reason for the apparent revival. Former Tsar Nicholas Alexandrovich and his family were to be transferred out of Tsarskoye Selo, and everything is ready for their departure, set to take place on August 1. But to where? That is unknown. It has been proposed that they go deep into Russia, to the Volga, to the city of Kostroma. Benckendorff and Obolensky, met us in the palace hall, and told us that tomorrow, Sunday, at about 2:00 p.m, after Divine Liturgy, it is proposed to serve a moleben before the miraculous icon, which is to be brought from the Znamensky Church. For this reason, we are to be detained for several hours. I asked, "What kind of moleben? For those about to travel?" To this he replied uncertainly, "Yes, it could be done so as to also be for those about to travel; but do it as you know best." What a surprise! By whose order? For what reason? And is this being done at their request or are they being compelled? No one can say. It is even unclear as to who will accompany, guard, and serve this formerly Imperial Family, now subjected to abuse, insult, and degradation, now helpless, now being taken from their family home, perhaps to travel far away into the wilderness, and into perhaps even greater sorrow and deprivation.

July 30, 1917 ~ Sunday. Former Heir Alexei Nikolaevich's birthday. After arriving at the palace at 10:00 a.m., we immediately went, under guard, straight to the church. None of those preparing to depart was in evidence. The valet came from the former Empress, bringing a small bunch of carnations, and said, "Her Majesty asks that you put these flowers on the icon of the Znamensky Mother of God,[28] which will be brought at 2:00 p.m. into the palace church. These flowers are to remain on the icon during the moleben, and then returned to Her Majesty. She wishes to take them with her on her journey." He also announced that after Divine Liturgy, we would be served lunch in Marie Feodorovna's apartment, while the members of the choir would have lunch in the little hall adjacent to the church. No other orders were given by anyone.

The liturgy began at 11:00 a.m.. Somehow, I could not help but feel that this was the last Divine Liturgy to be served in the former Tsar's dwelling, and that for the last time the former rulers of their own home had gathered to fervently pray, tearfully, and on bended knee, imploring that the Lord help and intercede for them in all of their sorrows and misfortunes. The entire Imperial Family, and their now extremely diminished number of servants attended the liturgy. By noon, the liturgy had concluded. On offering the cross for veneration, I gave my final homily on the Gospel reading, in which I said, among other things, that there is no greater love than that of parents for their children.

> To parents it does not matter what labors they take on, or what deprivation they might experience for their children, as long as they are to their children's benefit. But nowhere does this parental love express itself more greatly than when children are ill. How much pain is heard in a father's word "O Lord, have mercy on my son, he is suffering greatly." Or what a heart-rending cry emanated from the heart of the Canaanite mother who cried "Have mercy upon me, O Lord, my daughter is greatly tormented." The mother suffers more than the daughter, and asks that the Lord have mercy on her—the mother. And when our merciful God hears the prayer and raises the ill one from the bed, then who can describe the parents' joy? Grant, O Lord, that the children who experience the fruits of parental love, might also say, as the holy hierarch said of his mother, "May our right hand lose its cunning if we should ever forget thee, our dear mother." Now, spiritually celebrating the birthday of the righteous Alexei Nikolaevich, I am unable to find the words,

I am unable to express in words, that which my heart would like to say. But I am convinced of the truth of my words. The news moves from heart to heart, and I profoundly believe that even without words my heartfelt best wishes will be heard, will permeate the receptive ears of those who stand here and pray.

The former Tsarina wept, and the former Tsar was evidently troubled. Kissing the cross, Nicholas Alexandrovich said, "I thank you." The others came up and kissed the cross in silence. Thus ended my final service for the former Imperial Family in the Alexander Palace.

After the liturgy, a servant invited us to lunch. He also served at the table, giving us some kind of extremely greasy meat with potatoes, cold macaroni, prune compote, coffee, kvas [a fermented drink made from bread or fruit], a glass of some kind of red wine, one piece of black bread per person, and very small rolls.

At 1:30 p.m., without having received any orders, we decided that we would go meet the icon. In our vestments, and accompanied by the members of the choir, we went to the main entrance, but it turned out that the icon was being brought to the fourth entrance, which was locked. We went to the fourth entrance, and waited for the gates to be opened. About ten minutes later, the keys were located, the door was opened, and, to the singing of "As an unassailable fortress and a fountain of miracles," we met the icon at the gates. It was accompanied by Archpriest Speransky and by his deacon. We carried the icon in solemn procession along the palace corridors, and without removing it from the litter on which it had been carried, placed it in the center of the church nave. At the same time, the entire Royal Family, their retinue, the servants and the guards arrived. I put the carnations on the crown of the infant Saviour.

The moleben began. The Imperial Family knelt, on bended knees, at their usual places, and prayed fervently. The petitions, Epistle, and Gospel readings, and the prayer were those pertinent to the rite for those about to travel, while the troparion, refrains, and a second prayer were taken from the moleben to the Mother of God. The moleben ended with the singing of "Many years" for the Russian Power, its government, armed forces, and for all those who stood in prayer in the church. Then, the former Sovereign silently approached me for a blessing. He was followed by his spouse, his daughters, and the former Heir. The

Archpriest Afanasy J. Belyaev

Fig. 2 The first page of Fr Afanasy's hand written diary, dated March 2, 1917, the day of his first visit to the Alexander Palace when Empress Alexandra requested that the Icon of the Sign be brought for a prayer service for the children. The Tsar had not yet returned following his abdication.

Fig. 3 Contemporary photo of the restored Feodorovsky Cathedral in Tsarskoye Selo. Commissioned by Nicholas II as a parish church for the military garrison on duty there, it was completed in 1910. Fr Afanasy was rector of the cathedral in 1917 when he was called to the palace to minister to the former Tsar and his family.

Fig. 4 Portrait of Nicholas II painted from life at Tsarskoye Selo in 1897
by Ernst Lipgart. Oil on canvas, set in its original gilt wood frame.

Fig. 5 Pierre Gilliard, French tutor, with two of his students, Grand Duchesses Olga and Tatiana, at Livadia, the family villa in the Crimea.

Fig. 6 Colonnade facade and right wing of the Alexander Palace. It is currently undergoing complete restoration. The family apartments of the last Tsar were located in the left wing of the palace.

Fig. 7 The family wing of the Alexander Palace. A modern automobile from the tsar's fleet stands in front.

Fig. 8 Aerial view of Tsarskoye Selo and the Catherine Palace.
The Alexander Palace is seen in part in the top right corner.

Fig. 9 The empress's Corner Reception Room in the Alexander Palace.

Fig. 10 Nicholas II seated on the empress's balcony, the Alexander Palace, reading a document.

Выходъ Его Императорскаго Величества Государя Императора на балконъ
Зимняго дворца къ народу послѣ молебствія 20-г Іюля 1914 г.

Fig. 11 Emperor Nicholas II on the balcony of the Winter Palace
following the moleben and announcement of the war, July 20, 1914.

Fig. 12 Contemporary photo of the restored Winter Palace.

„БОЖЕ, ЦАРЯ ХРАНИ!"

Въ день объявленія войны передъ Зимнимъ Дворцомъ.

РѢЧЬ ГОСУДАРЯ ИМПЕРАТОРА,
20-го Іюля 1914 г. ВЪ ЗИМНЕМЪ ДВОРЦѢ:

„Со спокойствіемъ и достоинствомъ встрѣтила наша Великая Матушка Русь извѣстіе объ объявленіи намъ войны. Убѣжденъ, что съ такимъ же чувствомъ спокойствія мы доведмъ войну, какая бы она ни была, до конца.

Я здѣсь торжественно заявляю, что не заключу мира до тѣхъ поръ, пока послѣдній непріятельскій воинъ не уйдетъ съ земли Нашей. И къ вамъ, собраннымъ здѣсь представителямъ дорогихъ Мнѣ войскъ гвардіи и Петербургскаго военнаго округа и въ вашемъ лицѣ, обращаюсь Я ко всей единородной, единодушной, крѣпкой, какъ стѣна гранитная, арміи Моей и благословлю ее на трудъ ратный".

Fig. 13 Postcard of the emperor's speech from the balcony of the Winter Palace to the assembled crowds below, July 20, 1914.

Fig. 14 Emperor Nicholas II, center left, conversing with Infantry General N. V. Ruzsky, center right, at General Headquarters, at Baronovichi, 1914. Lt General N. N. Yanushkevich, Chief of General Staff, center.

Fig. 15 Tsarevich Alexei outside the rear exit of the Alexander Palace, at the start of a sleigh ride.

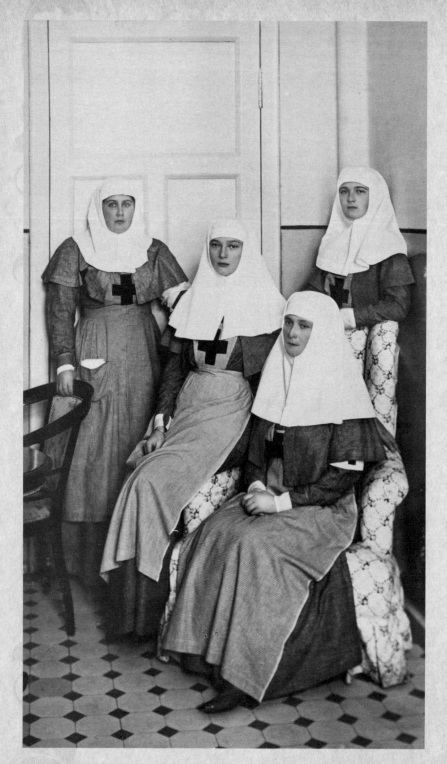

Fig. 16 Empress Alexandra Feodorovna, seated, and daughters Grand Duchesses Tatiana, left, and Olga, standing right, with Anna Vyrubova, far left, in the infirmary hospital where they worked as Red Cross nurses. Tsarskoye Selo, 1916.

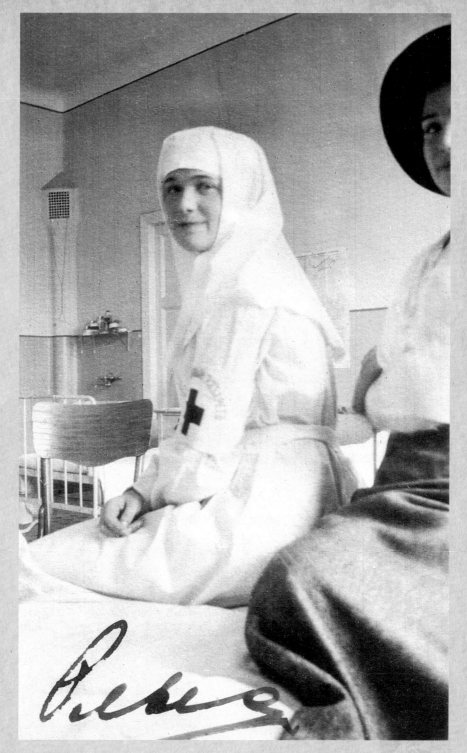

Fig. 17 Grand Duchess Olga in a hospital room of the empress's infirmary. Tsarskoye Selo, 1915–16.

Ставка

Начальнику Штаба.

Въ дни великой борьбы съ внѣшнимъ врагомъ,стремящимся
почти три года поработить нашу родину,Господу Богу угодно
было ниспослать Россіи новое тяжкое испытаніе.Начавшіяся
внутреннія народныя волненія грозятъ бѣдственно отразиться
на дальнѣйшемъ веденіи упорной войны.Судьба Россіи,честь
геройской нашей арміи,благо народа,все будущее дорогого на-
шего Отечества требуютъ доведенія войны во что бы то ни
стало до побѣднаго конца.Жестокій врагъ напрягаетъ послѣд-
нія силы и уже близокъ часъ,когда доблестная армія наша
совмѣстно со славными нашими союзниками сможетъ окончатель-
но сломить врага.Въ эти рѣшительные дни въ жизни Россіи,
почли МЫ долгомъ совѣсти облегчить народу НАШЕМУ тѣсное
единеніе и сплоченіе всѣхъ силъ народныхъ для скорѣйшаго
достиженія побѣды и,въ согласіи съ Государственною Думою,
признали МЫ за благо отречься отъ Престола Государства Рос-
сійскаго и сложить съ СЕБЯ Верховную власть.Не желая рас-
статься съ любимымъ Сыномъ НАШИМЪ,МЫ передаемъ наслѣдіе
НАШЕ Брату НАШЕМУ Великому Князю МИХАИЛУ АЛЕКСАНДРОВИЧУ и
благословляемъ Его на вступленіе на Престолъ Государства
Россійскаго.Заповѣдуемъ Брату НАШЕМУ править дѣлами госу-
дарственными въ полномъ и ненарушимомъ единеніи съ предста-
вителями народа въ законодательныхъ учрежденіяхъ,на тѣхъ
началахъ,кои будутъ ими установлены,принеся въ томъ ненa-
рушимую присягу.Во имя горячо любимой родины призываемъ
всѣхъ вѣрныхъ сыновъ Отечества къ исполненію своего свято-
го долга передъ Нимъ,повиновеніемъ Царю въ тяжелую минуту
всенародныхъ испытаній и помочь ЕМУ,вмѣстѣ съ представите-
лями народа,вывести Государство Россійское на путь побѣды,
благоденствія и славы.Да поможетъ Господь Богъ Россіи.

Г.Псковъ.
2ᵍ Марта 15 час. 5 мин.1917 г.

Fig. 18 Photo of Nicholas II in a window of the Imperial train, 1916. He is seen wearing the Order of St George, Russia's highest military order, presented to him in November 1915 by the Southern Army.

Fig. 19 Document of Abdication of Nicholas II, dated March 15, 1917. Signed simply "Nicholas", it is countersigned according to court protocol by Count Vladimir Fredericks, minister of the Imperial Court.

Fig. 20 Nicholas II during a walk in the Alexander Park. Spring 1917.

Fig. 21 The family and household preparing the vegetable garden outside the Alexander Palace. Grand Duchess Tatiana, center, carries soil with Baroness Buxhoeveden, left. Spring 1917.

Fig. 22 Empress Alexandra Feodorovna and Grand Duchess Tatiana on a carriage ride in the Alexander Park. Spring 1917.

Fig. 23 Grand Duchess Olga on a bicycle ride in the Alexander Park.
Spring 1917.

Fig. 24 Nicholas II walking with his daughters, left to right, Grand
Duchesses Tatiana, Anastasia, Maria, and Olga.
Spring 1917.

Fig. 25 Watercolor of spring crocuses on a postcard, painted by Grand Duchess Maria Nikolaevna. Signed and dated MN 1913. On the reverse is a note written by Grand Duchess Maria from Tobolsk in 1917: *15 August 1917, Dear Vera Vladimirovna,*
Thank you from my heart for your good wishes. I hope you have recovered completely. It is so sad to be ill in the summer when one wants to be outside in the fresh air.
With my love and best wishes, M.

Fig. 26 Prayer card painted by Empress Alexandra in Tobolsk in 1917. Artistically written in Old Church Slavonic, is a verse from Psalm 34:18 (Psalm 33:19 LXX): "The Lord is near those who have a broken heart, And saves such as have a contrite spirit."

Fig. 27 Prayer card painted by Empress Alexandra in Tobolsk in 1918. Artistically decorated in Art Nouveau style with a swastika, an ancient Eastern symbol found in the catacombs of the early Christians, is a verse from Psalm 103:8-9: "The Lord is compassionate and gracious, long suffering and abounding in mercy. He will not always strive with us, Nor will He keep His anger forever."

Fig. 28 Empress Alexandra Feodorovna with her needlework during an outing in the Alexander Park. Ground prepared for the vegetable garden can be seen behind her. Spring 1917.

Fig. 29 The miraculous Icon of the Sign taken by Fr Afanasy to the Alexander Palace twice during the house arrest of the Tsar and his family in 1917.

Fig. 30 The Icon of the Sign being carried in procession to the Alexander Palace, passing the Catherine Palace at right. Spring 1917. The photographer is the tutor Sydney Gibbes.

Fig. 31 The Governor's House in Tobolsk, left. The Church of the Annunciation is seen, right, in back.

Fig. 32 The tsar's study in the Governor's House, Tobolsk.

Fig 33 The Tsar and his son, Alexei, sawing wood in the yard of the Governor's House in Tobolsk, 1917–18.

Fig. 34 The empress's sitting room in the Governor's House, Tobolsk.

Fig. 35 The Church of the Annunciation, Tobolsk. Winter 1917–18.

Fig. 36 The open carriage in which Nicholas II, Empress Alexandra, and Grand Duchess Maria were transported on the arduous trip to Tyumen at the start of the journey to Ekaterinburg. Tobolsk, March 1918.

Fig. 37 Prayer card written in French with a verse from the writings of St. Teresa of Avila: "Let nothing disturb you, Let nothing frighten you, All things are passing; God alone is changeless. Patience gains all things. Who has God wants nothing else, God alone suffices." Accompanying the card is a letter of the Empress to her friend, Lili Dehn.

Thank you so much for your wishes on my namesday. Thoughts & prayers always with you, poor suffering creature! Her M. read to us all your lines; horrid to think all you had to go through! We are alright here — it is quite quiet. Pity you are not with us. Kisses & blessings without end from your loving friend.

A.

Give my best love to y⁻ parents.

Dec. 1ˢᵗ

Fig. 38 A Thank You Note of Nicholas II to Anna Vyrubova.

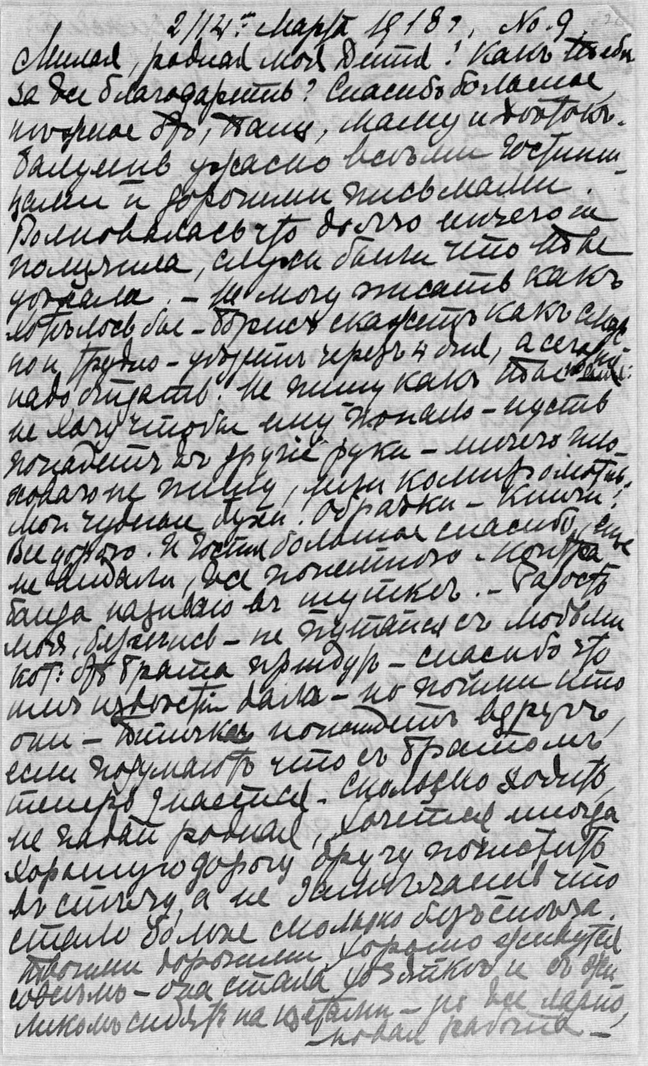

Fig. 39 Letter of Empress Alexandra to Anna Vyrubova, 2/14 March 1918. Written in Tobolsk shortly before the journey to Ekaterinburg, it is perhaps her last letter to Anna. See translated excerpt below.

2/14 March, 1918.

No. 9

My darling child,

…I worry so much. My God, how Russia suffers! You know that I love it even more than you do, miserable country, demolished from within and by the Germans from without. Since the Revolution, they have conquered a great deal of it without even a battle… If they created order now in Russia how dreadful would be the country's de-basement—to have to be grateful to the enemy.

We hope to go to Communion next week, if they allow us to go to church. On the whole we are better off than you. It will soon be a year since we parted, but what is time? Life here is nothing, eternity everything, and what we are doing by suffering is preparing our souls for the Kingdom of Heaven.

Thus nothing, after all, is terrible, and if they do take everything from us they cannot take our souls….

…What a nightmare it is that it is the Germans who are saving Russia [from Communism] and are restoring order. What could be more humiliating for us? With one hand the Germans give, and with the other they take away. Already they have seized an enormous territory. God help and save this unhappy country. Probably He wills us to endure all these insults, but that we must take them from the Germans almost kills me. Now Batoum has been taken—our country is disintegrating into bits. I cannot think calmly about it. Such hideous pain in heart and soul. Yet I am sure God will not leave it like this. He will send wisdom and save Russia I am sure….

Fig. 40 The chapel set up in the ballroom of the Governor's House in Tobolsk when the family was no longer allowed to go to the nearby church. Winter 1917–18.

Fig. 41 Liturgy in the chapel created in the ballroom of the Governor's House, Tobolsk. The priest from the Annunciation Church serves with a choir of nuns from a local monastery, seen far right.

Fig. 42 Icon of the Holy Royal Martyrs, Tsar Nicholas II, Tsarina Alexandra, Tsarevich Alexei, Grand Duchesses Olga, Tatiana, Maria, and Anastasia. Painted by Archimandrite Cyprian (Pyshov) of Holy Trinity Monastery, Jordanville, New York.

Fig. 43 Prayer card painted by Empress Alexandra in Tobolsk in 1918 with a Troparion which she copied from the Orthodox Funeral Service: "O Thou Who, with wisdom profound, mercifully orderest all things and Who gives that which is expedient unto all men, O only Creator, give rest, O Lord, to the souls of Thy servants who have fallen asleep; for they have set their hope on Thee, our Maker, the Author of our being, and our God."

Fig. 44 Icon of the New Martyrs of Russia killed at the hands of the godless. Painted by Archimandrite Cyprian (Pyshov) of Holy Trinity Monastery, Jordanville, New York.

soldiers who had carried the icon lifted it onto their shoulders, and took it through the Semi-Circular Hall and into the park. It was followed by the clergy, choir, and by the Imperial Family onto the balcony, and to the steps descending to the park, where they stopped. The icon moved on, while we, returning to the church, bowed down for the final time before the former Tsar and his family. Taking off our vestments, we left the altar, and found ourselves alone. Everyone had gone their own way. The guard accompanied us to the gates of the park, where three carriages had been provided: one for me, one for the protodeacon and the chanter, and one for the four choir members. Thus, my five months' service in the Alexander Palace church and for the imprisoned family of the ruling house of the Romanovs, ended in silence, unnoticed, but, I can say with a clear conscience, not without a trace.

August 1, 1917 ~ At 5:45 a.m., the Alexander Palace was emptied of its residents. No one slept all night. The night was troubled. Toward morning, automobiles were furnished, and the entire former Imperial Family, tortured by long anticipation, finally and tearfully said goodbye to its home, and set out on a road into a distant and unexplored wilderness, into cold Siberia.

August 2, 1917 ~ A newspaper account appeared stating that the Romanov family had left for Tobolsk.

August 3, 1917 ~ Thursday. At noon, Count Benckendorff came to my apartment and brought with him in a carrying case a crystal pectoral cross framed in gold and on a gold chain. Giving me the cross, the Count said, "Their Majesties, the former Sovereign and the former Empress, have asked me to give you this cross in remembrance of them, and in thanks for your excellent zealous service, for your comforting words and instructions, which so deeply penetrated into their hearts and had such a calming effect upon them. They express these heartfelt thanks both from themselves and on behalf of their children. They ask your prayers, of which they have such need and through which they hope to find happiness and comfort."

He also told me that the last night on the eve of August first was very sad and extremely difficult for all of those who were to travel. Orders were given to be ready to leave at 1:00 a.m., but they had to wait, exhausted and dressed for travel, until 6:00 a.m. Three days before their departure they learned that the Provisional Government had decided to transfer the former Tsar out of Tsarskoye Selo. But where? It was unknown. They asked to go south, to Crimea, and they, especially the children, were overjoyed to hear that they would be freed of their strict confinement. But when they were told that they should take warm clothing, they guessed to their horror that they were going north. When they learned that they were to take five days' provisions, they began to surmise, to their greater horror, that their place of exile was to be Tobolsk. In tears, they left their family home. The following persons voluntarily accompanied them: Prince Dolgorukov, Dr Botkin, the French teacher, Gendrikova, Schneider, and the nannies. All told, counting the servants, there were about fifty people. The Sovereign's final words were "I do not feel sorry for myself, but I feel sorry for those people who because of me have suffered and are suffering. I feel sorry for the homeland and the people."

Epilogue

By mid-July, Alexander Kerensky had decided that it was time for the family to leave Tsarskoye Selo for the "safety" of Siberia. He selected as their destination the town of Tobolsk, a provincial backwater of 20,000 people in western Siberia.

Founded by Cossacks in the late sixteenth century, Tobolsk sits high above the Irtysh River. It is 200 miles north of the Trans-Siberian Railway line and could only be reached by boat. Dominating the lower part of the town is a mansion in provincial neoclassical style built in 1788 by a local merchant. It was taken over by the government in 1817 to be the residence of the governor-general of the region. It was here that the last tsar and his family were brought in August 1917.

The journey to Tobolsk commenced early on the morning of August 1. The family, along with an entourage of thirty-nine attendants, retainers, and aides, was taken to the local Alexandrovka station to board the train that would take them to Tyumen. There they would be transferred to a steamer for the remainder of the journey. Nicholas recorded the moment of their departure in his diary: "There was a beautiful sunrise as we set out along the branch line of the northern railway. We left Tsarskoye Selo at 6:10 in the morning."[29]

They arrived at Tyumen on August 3 at midnight and were transferred along with their entourage to steamers for the forty-hour voyage to Tobolsk. Arriving on August 6, they spent another week on board while the Governor's House was made ready. The house, although large, was unostentatious, white, and balconied. Consisting of two stories and thirteen or fourteen rooms, it stood prominently on a dusty street named Liberty Street. The family would occupy the whole of the upper floor for the next eight months.

Most of the entourage that accompanied them had to stay in a house across the street. They were allowed to cross over to the Governor's House, but no one from the Imperial Family could cross over to them.

The prisoners settled into a regular routine. The younger Grand Duchesses, Maria and Anastasia, and Alexei continued the lessons given by their parents and the two devoted tutors who followed the family into exile: Sydney Gibbes, the English tutor, and Pierre Gilliard, the Swiss citizen who taught them French. Alexandra read, embroidered, or painted. Nicholas walked in the compound whenever he could or sawed logs strenuously with anyone who would join him. This was usually Alexei.

People in Tobolsk were warm and loyal whenever they saw a member of the family. Some would kneel when Nicholas and Alexandra walked to the nearby Annunciation Church for a service, even though they were flanked by soldiers. These trips were permitted in the beginning of their stay in Tobolsk. Some would make the sign of the cross when one of them appeared at a window. Gifts of food came from the town and nuns from a nearby convent brought eggs and sugar. Life was reasonably serene in the beginning.

But by the end of the year, things began to change. The Provisional Government was overthrown by the Bolsheviks in October and terror began to stalk the country as Red Guards advanced. Tobolsk was momentarily forgotten in the icy cold of the winter. Although there were fireplaces in the rooms, it could be frigid in the house. "One lives from day to day," Alexandra wrote in one of her letters smuggled out to her friend, Anna Vyrubova. "... God have mercy and save Russia."[30]

The mounting danger drew them all closer together.

In December, they were no longer permitted to attend church services because the deacon had intoned the customary prayer for the emperor and his family, by name, during a service. The Bolsheviks were in charge of Tobolsk by then and the family's privilege of going to church was withdrawn. They improvised a chapel in the ballroom of the house for services. An altar was set up with Alexandra's white lace bedspread as an altar cloth. The priest from the Annunciation Church would come to officiate and a few local nuns were the choir. But a soldier always had to be present at any service.

By day, they would keep to their essential routine. But they had to find some way to get through the bleak evenings. The coming of Christmas that winter, which was to be their last, became a time of special planning. Under house arrest and now closely guarded, it was quite different from all previous Christmases at home in the Alexander Palace.

With thoughtful planning, they organized a traditional Christmas that in many ways became their closest family holiday. The simplicity, warmth, and resourcefulness they displayed in the face of deprivation and humiliation was a triumph of the human spirit over adversity.

Olga Nikolaevna left a vivid description of that last Christmas in a letter to one of her friends.

> *December 26, 1917 Tobolsk*
> *Dear Rita,*
>
> *We have here in the hall, a Christmas tree with a wonderful scent, completely unlike anything we had in Tsarskoye. It is a "balsam evergreen." It has a strong scent like mandarin orange blossom and the trunk emits resin. There are no decorations, only silver tinsel and wax candles—from the church of course. After supper on Christmas Eve we organized the presents, most of which were things we sewed. The vigil service took place around ten o'clock in the evening. The Christmas tree was lit. It was beautiful and cozy. There was a large choir and they sang well, but it was too much like a concert and this I don't like... Papa and the children are now having coffee. Mama is not up yet. The sun is out and shines over my right shoulder...*
>
> *Wishing you much happiness in the coming year, with hugs and love to you, my dear friend. God bless you,*
> *Your Olga"*[31]

Pierre Gilliard described in his memoirs the wonderful spirit of that memorable Christmas. "It felt as though we had become one big family. We began to forget all our cares and sorrows and to enjoy ourselves, not thinking of anything else in these moments of pure friendship, in complete unity of heart."[32]

Nicholas noted in his diary on Christmas morning the additional blessing of "a moleben served after liturgy in front of the miraculous Abalakskaya Icon of the Mother of God[33] which had been brought the evening before from the monastery twenty-four versts from here."

While the family was still in Tobolsk, Nicholas conveyed what would be his final message to the Russian people in a letter written by his oldest daughter, Olga, to a friend. "Father asks to have it passed on to all who have remained loyal to him and to those on whom they might have influence, that they not avenge him; he has forgiven and prays for everyone; and not to avenge themselves, but to remember that the evil which is now in the world will become yet more powerful, and that it is not evil which conquers evil, but only love…"[34]

The family remained in custody in Tobolsk until April 1918 when a mysterious agent arrived from Moscow. Sent by M. Sverdlov and the Central Committee, Vasily Yakovlev had been charged with transferring the former tsar and his family to Moscow. Plans to put Nicholas on trial had been discussed right from the beginning when Lenin had come to power. Yakovlev, however, never revealed their planned destination.

Alexei was too ill to travel, having taken a fall that aggravated his hemophilia. It was decided that Nicholas would be taken accompanied by Alexandra and their daughter Maria. They set off at four o'clock in the morning on April 22 in an open cart for the long and arduous trip in the early spring thaw. It was nearly 200 miles to Tyumen and then further by train.

Along the way, the train was intercepted by the Ekaterinburg Bolsheviks who took control and directed the train east to Ekaterinburg, their final destination. The Urals were a stronghold of radical socialism and Ekaterinburg was the central city of the Bolsheviks in that region. The mood of the local population was harshly against the former tsar, quite different from the respectful recognition of Tobolsk.

Nicholas, Alexandra, and Maria arrived in Ekaterinburg on April 30, 1918. They were taken to another requisitioned house, that of a local engineer, Nikolai Ipatiev. The harsh conditions inside the "House of Special Purpose" as it was called, resembled a prison regime. In the new language of hatred and class violence that emerged with the Bolshevik regime, the prisoners were "enemies of the people."

On May 23, soon after Pascha, the rest of the children and the loyal attendants who accompanied them, arrived in Ekaterinburg. For their two remaining months, they all lived in these brutal conditions. Windows were whitewashed and sealed. Only one was allowed to remain open during the hot months to follow. The special Red Guard recruited from local factory workers was intrusive everywhere in their living quarters.

By the end of June, anti-Bolshevik forces were moving closer to the area. It was decided in Moscow that in view of a military threat against Ekaterinburg, execution of the former tsar, without a trial, could not be put off. It is now generally confirmed that Lenin gave the final approval for the execution.

At the beginning of July, a new commandant, Jacob Yurovsky, was assigned to the House of Special Purpose. He would head the team of executioners on July 17 in the brutal murder of the family and the attendants who were with them: Dr Eugene Botkin; the maid, Anna Demidova; the valet, Alexei Trupp; and the cook, Ivan Kharitonov. The tutors, Sydney Gibbes and Pierre Gilliard, were released, as they were not Russian citizens.

On Sunday, July 14, a local priest, Fr John Storozhev, and his deacon were allowed to come to the Ipatiev House and serve liturgy. The family gathered silently in the dining room. A guard stood in attendance in the background. The priest and his deacon were not allowed to speak to the former tsar or his family. But one of the daughters whispered a barely audible "thank you" as they passed on their way out after the service. "Something has happened with them there," the deacon said to his priest as they left the house. They were both struck by how different the family appeared.[35]

Three days later they were all awakened around 1:00 a.m. Told to get dressed, they were taken down to a room in the cellar "for safety." Lined up as if for a photograph, they were brutally gunned down and bayoneted by the team of executioners who entered the room. The bodies were taken to a waiting Fiat truck and transported to an abandoned mine shaft about twenty kilometers away. Later that night, Yurovsky returned to the mine shaft, fearing that the location of their burial was not sufficiently remote. He ordered that they be removed to another location. Along the way, the truck got stuck in the mud and it was decided to bury them on the spot. The Bolsheviks tried to burn two of them, Alexei and one of the girls, but were unable to complete the task. They were buried nearby. There they would all remain for the next fifty years.

The main burial site was discovered in the 1970s, but it was not until the fall of communism that the skeletons could be exhumed and identified.

In the 1990s, word spread in the West that skeletal remains found near Ekaterinburg could be those of the last tsar and his family. These were tested in forensic laboratories in Europe, America, and Russia using the new technology of DNA. The DNA of numerous living Romanov relatives, including members of the British royal family, was compared with the DNA extracted from the skeletal remains in Ekaterinburg. The results were conclusively a match in every case.

Although the Russian Orthodox Church has not yet confirmed the authenticity of the skeletal remains, the Russian Federation, under Boris Yeltsin, brought them from Ekaterinburg to St Petersburg on July 17, 1998, for burial in the Saints Peter and Paul Cathedral, the traditional burial site of the Romanov sovereigns. The Imperial Family and those who were killed with them were buried together in the St Catherine chapel within the main cathedral. Alexei and Maria, whose remains had not yet been found, were missing.

Much earlier, on November 1, 1981, in New York, the Imperial Family and those killed with them were canonized among the New Martyrs and Confessors of Russia by the Russian Orthodox Church Outside Russia.

On August 20, 2000, the Russian Orthodox Church under the Moscow-based patriarchate canonized the last tsar and his family with the New Martyrs and Confessors of Russia in the twentieth century in Moscow following the consecration of the rebuilt Cathedral of Christ the Saviour. Those who were killed with them in Ekaterinburg were not included. But more recently, Dr Eugene Botkin, their loyal physician who remained with them, was canonized on February 26, 2016.

In recent years, a remarkable veneration of the last tsar and his family has developed in Russia. Icons of the Royal Martyrs are seen in numerous churches. Monuments to Nicholas II have been placed in cities all across Russia: St Petersburg, Moscow, Ekaterinburg, Kursk, Kaluga, Novosibirsk, Sochi, Sevastopol, Yalta, and Vladivostok, as well as in Belgrade, Serbia.

Thousands of pilgrims come to Ekaterinburg each year to attend the midnight liturgy on July 17 served at the church built on the site of the Ipatiev House. More than 60,000 people came in the centennial year, 2017, for the midnight liturgy and the thirteen-mile religious procession to Ganina Yama where the bodies were first brought. A monastery is there now, dedicated to the Holy Royal Martyrs.

The memorable words of Fr Alexander Shargunov on the day of the canonization in Moscow in 2000, were prophetic: "In 1917, our Tsar was taken from us. Today, he has returned."[36]

Acknowledgments

Holy Trinity Publications would like to thank the Recovery Foundation (Возрожденіе) in Washington, DC, and its director, Eugene Vernigora, for giving permission to use the translation the foundation prepared in honor of its spiritual patron, the Tsar Martyr Nicholas II.

It was Eugene Vernigora who found the diary in the State Archive of the Russian Federation (GARF) and, recognizing its significance, brought it to the Recovery Foundation. Fr Victor Potapov and Matushka Maria Potapov encouraged the foundation to publish the diary of Fr Afanasy in both English and Russian. A blessing for the work was given by the Most Reverend Archbishop Laurus (Škurla). The foundation arranged for Protodeacon Leonid Michailistschenko to translate the work into English and for Marilyn Pfeifer Swezey to edit it for publication. In 2004, a portion of the diary of Fr Afanasy appeared in the journal *Pravoslavnaya Rus'* in the Russian language and in the journal *Orthodox Life* in the English language.

We are also grateful to Marilyn Pfeifer Swezey who, inspired by the witness of the Russian Royal Family, brought the concept for this book to Holy Trinity Publications, completed the manuscript to give a full picture to the reader, and selected the photos. Her work, love, care, and enthusiasm in preparing the manuscript for publication was essential and a testament to her own profound love for the Royal Martyrs of Russia.

Appendix 1

A Biography of Archpriest Afanasy I. Belyaev

Mitred Archpriest Afanasy Ioanovich Belyaev, rector of the tsar's Feodorovsky Cathedral, Tsarskoye Selo, was chaplain and confessor to Nicholas II and his family in the Alexander Palace during the period of their house arrest, March through August 1917.

Fr Afanasy was born into a priest's family in St Petersburg on February 15 /27, 1845.[37] He completed the St Petersburg Ecclesiastical Seminary in June 1865. Following his marriage, he was ordained to the priesthood on January 15/27, 1868, and served at the Church of the Transfiguration in Moscow Slovyanka in the administrative region of Tsarskoye Selo.

From 1868 to 1919, Fr Afanasy was responsible for teaching religion in various regional schools: the Moscow Slovyanka Zemstvo School, the Moscow Slovyanka Parish School, the Tsarskoye Selo St Catherine Parish School, the Tsarskoye Selo Zemstvo School, the school of the 37th Artillery Brigade, the Artillery Factories of Ijorsk, the Sunday School of the Ladies of the Union of October 17 of Tsarskoye Selo, the Shelter School of the Grand Duchess Marie Alexandrovna, the Shelter of Alexander Nevsky, the School of Levitsky, and the Konvoy of His Imperial Highness.

In 1887 he was one of the candidates nominated for management of the Alexander Nevsky Ecclesiastical Seminary and appointed a member of the commission to review the books that were nominated for the Peter I Prize in 1889.

For nine years he was elected by the clergy to be the assistant to the regional dean of the administrative center of Tsarskoye Selo.

In 1895 he became a member of the Prison Department and the Institution for Sobriety. He was elected to chair the Ecclesiastical Old Age Fund for the Diocese of St Petersburg and was appointed to oversee the teaching of religion in the School of the Ministries and the Zemstvo. Archpriest Afanasy was also an honorary member of the Brotherhood of the Holy Mother of God.

On February 24/March 9, 1904, Archpriest Afanasy was elevated to the nobility by the Ruling Senate.

On October 24/November 6, 1916, he was appointed rector of the tsar's Feodorovsky Cathedral. This appointment was later confirmed to include the additional responsibility of garrison priest of Tsarskoye Selo.

On April 27/March 12, 1917, after the Bolshevik Revolution, he was invited to the Alexander Palace to serve in the palace church. Nicholas II requested him to become the confessor of the tsar's family. From March 2/15 to August 2/15, he conducted all the religious services in the Alexander Palace during the house arrest of the Imperial Family in Tsarskoye Selo.

Fr Afanasy died on October 21, 1921, and is buried in the cemetery of the village of Moscow Slovyanka.

Orders and Awards Received by Archpriest Afanasy

September 6 /18, 1889	Gold medal from the Ministry of Education
February 3/15, 1894	Order of St Anne, 3rd Class
February 26 /March 10, 1896	Medal commemorating the reign of Alexander III
May 6/18, 1896	Order of St Vladimir, 2nd Class
April 26 /May 9, 1901	Gold insignia of Empress Marie
May 6/19, 1905	Order of St Vladimir, 4th Class, and medal commemorating the Russo-Japanese War
May 6/19, 1906	Order of St Vladimir 3rd Class
1910	Insignia of the 200th anniversary of Tsarskoye Selo
May 6/19, 1912	Order of St Anne, 1st Class
March 20/2 April, 1913	Insignia commemorating the 300 years of rule of the Romanov Dynasty
May 6/19, 1915	Insignia of the Red Cross on behalf of Empress Marie Feodorovna and the Red Cross Headquarters in Russia, and Order of St Vladimir, 2nd Class
1916	Order of St Alexander Nevsky
October 1, 1919	Medal commemorating the establishment of parochial schools

Appendix 2

Persons of Interest

Alexandra Feodorovna (June 6, 1872–July 17, 1918) Empress of Russia, spouse of Nicholas II. She was killed in Ekaterinburg with her family on the night of July 16–17, 1918.

Alexei Nikolaevich (July 30, 1904–July 17, 1918) Tsarevich and heir to the throne, only son and youngest child of Nicholas II and Alexandra Feodorovna. He was killed in Ekaterinburg with his family on the night of July 16–17, 1918.

Anastasia Nikolaevna (June 5, 1901–July 17, 1918) Grand Duchess, the fourth child of Nicholas II and Alexandra Feodorovna. She was killed in Ekaterinburg with her family on the night of July 16–17, 1918.

Benckendorff, Paul Konstantinovich (1833–1921) Count, Marshal of the Imperial Court in Tsarskoye Selo, and member of the State Council. He was part of the inner circle of the Imperial Family.

Bogrov, Dmitry Grigorievich (1887–1911) Socialist revolutionary. He assassinated Russian Prime Minister Peter Stolypin in the Kiev opera house in the presence of Nicholas II and two of the Grand Duchesses.

Botkin, Eugene Sergeevich (1865–1918) Personal doctor to Nicholas II and his family. He accompanied the family into exile in Tobolsk and Ekaterinburg, and was killed with them on the night of July 16–17,1918.

Buxhoeveden, Sophie Karlovna (1884–1956) Baroness, lady-in-waiting to Empress Alexandra Feodorovna. She voluntarily followed the family to Tobolsk and accompanied the children on the journey to Ekaterinburg, but was not allowed to join them there. She lived the rest of her life in London. She is the author of three memoirs: *The Life and Tragedy of Alexandra Feodorovna* (1928), *Left Behind: Fourteen Months in Siberia During the Russian Revolution* (1929), and *Before the Storm* (1938).

Demidova, Anna Stepanovna (1878–1918) Housekeeper in service to the Imperial Family. She accompanied them to Tobolsk and Ekaterinburg, and was killed with them on the night of July 16–17, 1918.

Derevenko, Vladimir Nikolaevich (1879–1936) Court surgeon and physician assigned to treat Tsarevich Alexei in 1912. Derevenko and his family followed the Imperial Family to Ekaterinburg where he was able occasionally to treat the ailing Alexei in the Ipatiev House. Derevenko's son, Kolya, was one of Alexei's friends.

Dolgorukov, Vasily Alexandrovich (1868–1918) Prince, Major General, Marshal of the Court. He followed the family to Tobolsk, was imprisoned on arrival in Ekaterinburg, and executed on July 10, 1918.

Fredericks, Vladimir Borisovich (1838–1927) Count, member of the State Council, minister of the Imperial Court, and head of the Imperial household at the Alexander Palace. He was one of the closest and most trusted associates of Nicholas II. He immigrated to his native Finland, a former duchy of Russia, after the Bolshevik Revolution.

Gibbes, Charles Sydney (1876–1963) Englishman and English tutor to the children of Nicholas II from 1908. He followed the family into exile in Tobolsk and was among those accompanying the children to Ekaterinburg, where he was released by the Bolsheviks as non-Russian. Before returning to England, he underwent a religious conversion and became a Russian Orthodox monk and priest, Fr Nicholas Gibbes. He later established an Orthodox congregation in Oxford where he kept a number of icons and personal belongings of the Imperial Family.

Gilliard, Pierre Andreevich (1879–1962) Swiss citizen and French language tutor to Tsarevich Alexei. He followed the family into exile in Tobolsk but was prevented from continuing with the family to Ekaterinburg by the Bolsheviks. He returned to Switzerland in 1920. He is the author of a memoir, *Thirteen Years at the Russian Court* (1921).

Guchkov, Alexander Ivanovich (1862–1936) Founder of the Octobrist Party, member of the Provisional Government of the State Duma during the February Revolution. With Vasily Shulgin, he negotiated the abdication of Nicholas II on March 2, 1917. In opposition to Soviet power, he immigrated to Germany in 1918.

Grosvenor, Gilbert Hovey (1875–1966) First editor of the *National Geographic* magazine, considered to be the father of photojournalism. He traveled throughout Russia in 1914, and dedicated the entire November 1914 issue of the *National Geographic* to "Young Russia, Land of Promise."

Hendrikova, Anastasia Vasilievna (1887–1918) Countess, lady-in-waiting to Empress Alexandra. She followed the Imperial Family into exile, and was executed with Catherine Schneider in Perm on September 4, 1918.

Kerensky, Alexander Feodorovich (1881–1970) Politician, lawyer, member of the Socialist Revolutionary Party in the Duma in 1917, and member of the Provisional Government and Minister of Justice during the February Revolution. He emigrated in 1918 and eventually went to the United States.

Kharitonov, Ivan Mikhailovich (1870–1918) Cook at the court of Nicholas II. He followed the family into exile and was killed with them in Ekaterinburg on the night of July 16–17, 1918.

Lenin, Vladimir Ilyich Ulyanov (1870–1924) Founder of the Russian Communist Party and leader of the October Revolution. He initiated

the reign of terror and genocide of the clergy and faithful of the Russian
Orthodox Church as well as members of the Romanov family. He was the
first president of the Soviet Union.

Lohmann, Dmitry Nikolaevich (1868–1918) Colonel of the Combined
Imperial Guard (Convoy) at Tsarskoye Selo and churchwarden of the
tsar's Feodorovsky Cathedral.

Marie Feodorovna (1847–1928) Dowager Empress of Russia, mother of
Nicholas II. She was born Princess Dagmar of Denmark, wife of
Alexander III. She emigrated from Crimea to Denmark in 1919.

Maria Nikolaevna (1899–1918) Grand Duchess, third daughter of Nicholas
II and Alexandra Feodorovna. She was killed with her family in
Ekaterinburg on the night of July 16–17, 1918.

Michael Alexandrovich (1878–1918) Grand Duke, youngest brother of
Nicholas II. He declined to accept the throne when Nicholas abdicated in
his favor in 1917, and was arrested and exiled to Perm after the October
Revolution. He was killed by the Bolsheviks near Perm on the night of
June 12–13, 1918.

Nicholas Alexandrovich (1868–1918) Emperor of Russia, succeeding to the
throne after the death of his father, Alexander III, on October 20, 1894.
He married Princess Alix of Hesse-Darmstadt on November 14, 1894,
was crowned in Moscow on May 14, 1896, and abdicated on March 2,
1917. He was killed with his family in Ekaterinburg on the night of July
16–17, 1918.

Nicholas Nikolaevich (1856–1929) Grand Duke, grandson of Nicholas I,
cousin of Nicholas II. He was commander in chief of the Russian Army
in World War I until replaced by Nicholas II in August 1915. He became
commander of the Caucasus armies until he was forced to resign by the
Provisional Government. He emigrated in March 1919 and settled in
southern France.

Olga Nikolaevna (1895–1918) Grand Duchess, eldest daughter of Nicholas II and Alexandra Feodorovna. She was killed with her family in Ekaterinburg on the night of July 16–17, 1918.

Rodzianko, Michael Vladimirovich (1859–1924) Chairman of the third and fourth State Dumas, member of the conservative Octobrist Party. He was leader of the Provisional Committee of the State Duma during the February Revolution. After the October Revolution, he served with the White Army under General Anton Denikin. He immigrated to Yugoslavia in 1920, and is the author of privately published memoirs.

Ruzsky, Nicholas Vladimirovich (1854–1918) Adjutant General in the Imperial suite, personally negotiated the abdication of Nicholas II. He was killed by the Red Army in Piatigorsk in October 1918.

Sazonov, Sergei Dmitrievich (1860–1927) Diplomat, Minister of Foreign Affairs 1910–1916. He immigrated to France in 1918.

Sergei Alexandrovich (1865–1905) Grand Duke, son of Alexander II, uncle and advisor of Nicholas II. He married Princess Elizabeth of Hesse-Darmstadt, the future Grand Duchess Elizabeth Feodorovna, sister of the future Empress Alexandra Feodorovna, in 1884. Commander of the Imperial Preobrajensky Regiment, he was appointed governor-general of Moscow in 1891. On February 17, 1905, he was assassinated by a Socialist Revolutionary terrorist as his carriage was leaving the Kremlin.

Schneider, Catherine Adolphovna (1856–1918) Language tutor and reader to the Imperial children, she had taught Russian to the Hessian princesses, Elizabeth and Alix, before their marriages to Grand Duke Sergei Alexandrovich and Tsarevich Nicholas Alexandrovich, future Nicholas II, respectively. She followed the Imperial Family into exile and was killed together with Anastasia Hendrikova in Perm on September 4, 1918.

Shulgin, Vasily Vitalievich (1878–1976) Publicist, deputy to the second, third, and fourth State Dumas, and member of the Provisional Committee of the Duma. During the February Revolution, he negotiated with Guchkov the abdication of Nicholas II. He immigrated to Yugoslavia, was arrested by the Soviet NKVD in 1944, and was sent to prison in the Soviet Union. Freed in 1956, he remained in Vladimir. Author of memoirs.

Stolypin, Peter Arkadievich (1862–1911) Prime Minister of Russia, 1906–1911. One of the most important prerevolutionary statesmen, he planned a network of land and financial reforms to create an agrarian middle class. He was assassinated in Kiev in the presence of Nicholas II by a Socialist Revolutionary, Dmitry Bogrov, on September 13, 1911.

Storozhev, John Vladimirovich (1878–1927) Archpriest called to serve liturgy in the Ipatiev House for the imprisoned Imperial Family on Sunday, July 14, 1918, three days before they were all killed. Fr Storozhev died in China and was buried in the Russian cemetery in Harbin. His family later settled in Japan before eventually immigrating to the United States.

Sverdlov, Jacob Mikhailovich (1885–1919) Member of the Central Committee of the Bolshevik Party and associate of Lenin in the new Soviet state. He directed the Ural Regional Party in Ekaterinburg in 1917. After his death in 1919, Ekaterinburg was known as Sverdlovsk from 1924 to 1991.

Tatiana Nikolaevna (1897–1918) Grand Duchess, second daughter of Nicholas II and Alexandra Feodorovna. She was killed with the family in Ekaterinburg on the night of July 16–17, 1918.

Trupp, Alexei Yegorovich (1856–1918) Tsar's valet who accompanied the family into exile in Tobolsk and Ekaterinburg. He was killed with the family in Ekaterinburg on the night of July 16–17, 1918.

Vyrubova, Anna Alexandrovna Taneyeva (1884-1964) Lady-in-waiting and close friend of Tsarina Alexandra Feodorovna. Born Anna Alexandra Taneyeva into a family with Imperial connections, she became a la-dy-in-waiting in 1905 to the Tsarina who saw in Anna a kind hearted and pious friend. Anna married an officer in the Imperial Chancellery, Alexander Vyrubov, in 1907, but the marriage was annulled eighteen months later. Anna was taken under the wing of the Imperial family and joined them on their annual summer holidays on the imperial yacht,

Standart, 1911-1914. These trips were recorded in seven photograph albums now in the Beinecke Rare Book and Manuscript Library at Yale University. In January 1915 Anna was severely injured in a train accident which left her crippled for life. She was a resident in the Alexander Palace when Fr Afanasy came in 1917. On March 21,1917, still very ill with measles, she was arrested by the Provisional Government and taken to the Peter and Paul Fortress where she spent five months of harsh imprisonment. She later corresponded with the imprisoned family through carefully smuggled letters. Anna managed to get to Finland in exile in 1921. Her memoirs, *Memories of the Russian Court,* were published in Paris in 1922. They present a rare view of the home life of the last tsar and his family. Anna lived her last years in Helsinki where she died on July 20, 1964 at the age of 80.

Witte, Sergei Yuliyevich (1849–1915) Minister of Finance and Prime Minister under Nicholas II. One of the most important statesman of Russia, Witte was largely responsible for Russia's great economic and industrial development after 1905. He was also a leading figure in the formation of a constitutional government under the autocracy.

Yakovlev, Vasily Vasilievich (1886–1938) Bolshevik revolutionary active in the Urals. In the spring of 1918, he was appointed by the new Soviet regime to transport the Imperial Family from Tobolsk to Ekaterinburg.

Yurovsky, Jacob Mikhailovich (1878–1938) Bolshevik activist in the Urals. He was elected to the Ekaterinburg Soviet in 1917, and was appointed commandant of the Ipaticv House (House of Special Purpose) on July 4, 1918. He headed the team of executioners that killed the Imperial Family and their retainers on the night of July 16–17, 1918. He died in the Kremlin Hospital in 1938.

Notes

The Historical Setting

1. All dates shown reflect the Julian calendar in secular and Church use in Russia prior to the Bolshevik Revolution. From 1900 the difference was thirteen days. Thus January 9, 1905, in Russia would have been January 22 in America.

2. Diary of Princess Ekaterina Alexeevna Sviatopolk-Mirsky for 1904–1905 as quoted in translation in Mark D. Steinberg and Vladimir M. Khrustalev, *The Fall of the Romanovs* (New Haven and London: Yale University Press, 1995), 10.

3. Edward J. Bing, ed., *The Secret Letters of the Last Tsar, (Being the Confidential Correspondence Between Nicholas II and His Mother, Dowager Empress Marie Feodorovna)* (1938), 186–187, as quoted in Dominic Lieven, *Nicholas II: Twilight of the Empire* (New York: St. Martin's Press, 1993), 147.

4. Bing, *Secret Letters*, 187–188; Lieven, *Nicholas II*, 148.

5. Bing, *Secret Letters*, 197, 200–201, Lieven, *Nicholas II*, 151.

6. "La transformation économique de la Russie," Edmond Théry (Paris, 1914), as quoted in S. S. Oldenburg, *Last Tsar: Nicholas II, His Reign and His Russia*, vol. 3, of *The Duma Monarchy, 1907–1914* (Munich, 1949), English translation (Gulf Breeze, FL: Academic International Press, 1977) 145.

7. Gilbert Grosvenor, *National Geographic*, November 1914.

8. Helen Tolstoy, oral communication, summer 1981.

9. Discussed in Dominic Lieven, *Russia and the Origins of the First World War* (Macmillan, 1983) and Lieven, Nicholas II, 191.

10. M. V. Rodzianko, Declaration by the Provisional Government on assuming state power, February 28, 1917, as quoted in Lieven, *Nicholas II*, 84.

11. P. E. Shchegolev, ed., *The Abdication of Nicholas II* (Leningrad,1927), 147, as quoted in translation, and Lieven, *Nicholas II*, 232.

12. Diary of Nicholas II, March 2, 1917, as quoted in translation in Steinberg and Khrustalev, *The Fall of the Romanovs*, 107.

13. Stavka was the general headquarters of the administrative staff in Imperial Russia.

14. Nicholas II, farewell address, March 21, 1917, as quoted in Lieven, *Nicholas II*, 234.

15. "My Impressions of Nicholas II, 1917," excerpted from Alexander Kerensky, *Russia and History's Turning Point* (New York: Duell, Sloan and Pearce, 1965) reprinted in Paul Gilbert, ed., *Sovereign*, no. 3 (2016): 53–63.

16. Ibid.

17. Note of Grand Duchess Olga Nikolaevna on a postcard, Tsarskoye Selo, July 12, 1917, during the house arrest of the family. Private collection, United States .

18. Last letter of Nicholas II to his mother, Dowager Empress Marie Feodorovna, Tsarskoye Selo, July 1917, during the house arrest of the family. Hoover Institution, Stanford University, California.

19. Count Paul Benckendorff, *Last Days at Tsarskoye Selo,* personal notes and memories, translated by Maurice Baring, (London: William Heinemann Limited, 1927), 65.

The Diary of Father Afanasy

20. The miraculous icon of the Queen of Heaven is also referred to as The Icon of Our Lady of the Sign, or the Znamensky Mother of God. See the photo in the insert figure 29.

21. The epitaphion is a cloth icon of Christ's body being prepared for burial after the crucifixion. The text embroidered in the border is taken from the vespers of Great Saturday served on Great Friday: "The Noble Joseph, taking Thy most pure body down from the Tree and having wrapped it in pure linen and spices, laid it in a new tomb."

22. This hymn is part of the Exapostilarion of Great Friday. The full text is: "The Wise Thief didst Thou make worthy of Paradise, in a single moment, O Lord. By the wood of Thy Cross illumine me as well, and save me."

23. After abstaining from meat and diary products during Great Lent, it is a Russian Orthodox Christian custom to include on the Paschal festal table kulich, a rich egg bread, and pascha, a sweet creamy cheese the consistency of cheesecake.

24. Orthodox Christians dye hard boiled eggs red at Pascha. The red reminds one of the blood of Christ, the hard shell His sealed tomb, and the cracked egg—His resurrection.

25. The ambo is a raised platform in front of the holy doors of the icon screen. The "prayer beyond" is a prayer said before the final dismissal.

26. John 4:24

27. Matt 9:22

28. The miraculous icon of the Queen of Heaven is also referred to as The Icon of Our Lady of the Sign, or the Znamensky Mother of God. See the photo in the insert figure 29.

Epilogue

29. *Dnevniki Imperatora Nikolai II* [Diary of Nicholas II] (Moscow: Obrita, 1991), 646, from the entry of July 31, 1917, translated from Russian by Marilyn Pfeifer Swezey.

30. From a letter of Empress Alexandra Feodorovna to Anna Vyrubova, in English, Tobolsk, December 1917, as quoted in Anna Vyrubova, *Memories of the Russian Court* (New York: Macmillan, 1923), 313.

31. From a letter of Grand Duchess Olga Nikolaevna to Rita Hitrovo, Tobolsk, December 26, 1917, translated from Russian by Marilyn P. Swezey as quoted in *Letters of the Holy Royal Martyrs in Exile,* 2nd ed. (St Petersburg: podvorye of the Valaam Holy Transfiguration Monastery, 1996), 174.

32. Pierre Gilliard, *Thirteen Years at the Russian Court (Russia Observed)* (New York: Arno Press/The NY Times, 1970), 246.

33. The Abalakskaya Icon of the Mother of God of the Sign is Siberia's most venerated holy icon. Its name is taken from the Tatar village of Abalak, thirty kilometers from Tobolsk. The icon was painted for a new church in 1637 based on a vision that a pious widow had in a dream. It was later kept in a monastery founded on the site. Over time, the icon became famous for many miracles and cures. It was brought to the governor's house in Tobolsk for the liturgy on Christmas for the former tsar and his family in January 1918.

34. From a letter of Grand Duchess Olga Nikolaevna, Tobolsk, 1918, *Letters of the Holy Royal Martyrs in Exile,* 324, translated from Russian by Marilyn Pfeifer Swezey.

35. John F. O'Conor, translation and commentary, *The Sokolov Investigation* (New York: Robert Speller & Sons, 1971), 124.

36. Oral communication, Moscow, August 20, 2000.

Appendix 1

37. Prior to the Bolshevik Revolution Russia used the Julian calendar. The dates according to both the Gregorian and Julian calendars are given here.

Illustration Credits

Fig. 1 Alexander Gubenov, Archpriest Afanasy I. Belyaev, 2017. Pen and ink. Source: Holy Trinity Publications, Jordanville, New York.

Fig. 2 Scan. Page of the diary of Archpriest Afanasy Belyaev. State Archive of the Russian Federation, Moscow. Source: The Recovery Foundation (Vozrojdenie), Washington DC.

Fig. 3 Photographer Клеткин, The Feodorovsky Cathedral, 20 June 2014. Color photograph. Source: https://commons.wikimedia.org/wiki/File:Фёдоровский_собор_(Царское_село) 3.jpg.

Fig. 4 Ernst Lipgart, Portrait of Nicholas II, 1897. Oil on canvas. Source: Private collection, USA.

Fig. 5 Photographer unknown, Pierre Gilliard and his pupils Olga and Tatiana. Scan of photograph. ID: 1000151. Source: The Romanov Collection. Beinecke Rare Book and Manuscript Library, Yale University.

Fig. 6 Photographer Victor Karasev, At the Alexander Palace, 10 July 2015. Color photograph. ID: 74016976. Source: dreamstime.com.

Fig. 7 Photographer unknown, Front, private (Imperial) entrance to the Alexander Palace. Scan of photograph ID: 1000453. Source: The Romanov Collection. Beinecke Rare Book and Manuscript Library, Yale University.

Fig. 8 Photographer Aleksei Kazachok, Aerial view of the autumn Catherine Park. Color photograph. ID: 740260216. Source: Used under license from Shutterstock.com.

Fig. 9 Photographer unknown, The Empress's drawing room, the Alexander Palace. Scan of photograph. ID: 1000451. Source: The Romanov Collection. Beinecke Rare Book and Manuscript Library, Yale University.

Fig. 10   Photographer unknown, Nicholas reading on the Empress' balcony at Tsarskoye Selo. Scan of photograph. ID: 1000230. Source: The Romanov Collection. Beinecke Rare Book and Manuscript Library, Yale University.

Fig. 11   Photographer unknown, The Emperor on the balcony of the Winter Palace following the formal declaration of war, 1914 July 20. Scan of postcard. ID: 1000246. Source: The Romanov Collection. Beinecke Rare Book and Manuscript Library, Yale University.

Fig. 12   Photographer Valeri Potapova, View Winter Palace in Saint Petersburg. Russia. Color photograph. ID: 202241017. Source: Used under license from Shutterstock.com.

Fig. 13   Photographer unknown, "God save the Tsar"—postcard with the declaration of World War I, 20 July 1914. Scan of postcard. ID: 1000241. Source: The Romanov Collection. Beinecke Rare Book and Manuscript Library, Yale University.

Fig. 14   Photographer unknown, Nicholas with Generals Yanushkevitch and Ruzsky. Scan of photograph. ID: 1000344. Source: The Romanov Collection. Beinecke Rare Book and Manuscript Library, Yale University.

Fig. 15   Photographer unknown, Alexis in the back entrance of the Alexander Palace. Scan of photograph. ID: 1000289. Source: The Romanov Collection. Beinecke Rare Book and Manuscript Library, Yale University.

Fig. 16   Photographer unknown, Anna, Tatiana, the Empress, and Olga posing in Red Cross uniforms. Scan of photograph. ID: 1000342. Source: The Romanov Collection. Beinecke Rare Book and Manuscript Library, Yale University.

Fig. 17   Photographer unknown, Olga posing in Red Cross uniform. Scan of photograph. ID: 1000256. Source: The Romanov Collection. Beinecke Rare Book and Manuscript Library, Yale University.

Fig. 18   Photographer unknown, Nicholas II in a window of the Imperial train, 1916. State Archive of the Russian Federation, Moscow. Scan of photograph. Source: Holy Trinity Monastery, Jordanville, New York.

Fig. 19   The Document of Abdication of Nicholas II. Facsimile, George V. Lomonossoff, *Memoirs of the Russian revolution* (New York: The Rand School of Social Science, 1919), Scan of Facsimile. Source: Holy Trinity Monastery, Jordanville, New York.

Fig. 20   Photographer unknown, Nicholas. Scan of photograph. ID: 1000294. Source: The Romanov Collection. Beinecke Rare Book and Manuscript Library, Yale University.

Fig. 21   Photographer unknown, The Imperial spading the ground for a vegetable garden, April 1917. Scan of photograph. ID: 1000011. Source: The Romanov Collection. Beinecke Rare Book and Manuscript Library, Yale University.

Fig. 22 Photographer unknown, Tatiana and Alexandra in a carriage. Scan of photograph. ID: 1000295. Source: The Romanov Collection. Beinecke Rare Book and Manuscript Library, Yale University.

Fig. 23 Photographer unknown, Olga on a bicycle ride with Tatiana under arrest. Scan of photograph. ID: 1000296. Source: The Romanov Collection. Beinecke Rare Book and Manuscript Library, Yale University.

Fig. 24 Photographer unknown, Nicholas and his daughters under arrest. Scan of photograph. ID: 1000297. Source: The Romanov Collection. Beinecke Rare Book and Manuscript Library, Yale University.

Fig. 25 Grand Duchess Maria Nikolaevna, Spring crocuses, 1913. Watercolor. Source: Private collection, USA.

Fig. 26 Empress Alexandra Feodorovna, Psalm 34:18 (Psalm 33:19 LXX), 1917. Watercolor. Scan of card. Source: The Romanov Collection. Beinecke Rare Book and Manuscript Library, Yale University.

Fig. 27 Empress Alexandra Feodorovna, Psalm 103:8-9, 1918. Watercolor. Scan of card. Source: The Romanov Collection. Beinecke Rare Book and Manuscript Library, Yale University.

Fig. 28 Photographer unknown, Alexandra doing needlework in her wheelchair in the park of the Alexander Palace, Spring 1917. Scan of photograph. ID: 1000009. Source: The Romanov Collection. Beinecke Rare Book and Manuscript Library, Yale University.

Fig. 29 Iconographer unknown. The Mother of God of the Sign. Icon. Color Photograph. Source: https://www.svytieicons.com/ znamenie-carskoselskaja-bogorodica.

Fig. 30 Photographer Charles Sydney Gibbes, The Icon of the Sign being carried in procession, Spring 1917. Scan of photograph, author archive. Source: Private Collection, England.

Fig. 31 Photographer unknown, The Governor's House in Tobolsk. Scan of photograph. Source: The Romanov Collection. Beinecke Rare Book and Manuscript Library, Yale University.

Fig. 32 Photographer Charles Sydney Gibbes, The tsar's study in the Governor's House. Scan of photograph, author archive. Source: Private Collection, England.

Fig 33 Photographer unknown, The Tsar and his son, Alexei, sawing wood, 1917-18. Scan of photograph. Source: The Romanov Collection. Beinecke Rare Book and Manuscript Library, Yale University.

Fig. 34 Photographer Charles Sydney Gibbes, The empress's sitting room in the Governor's House, Tobolsk. Scan of photograph, author archive. Source: Private Collection, England.

Fig. 35   Photographer Charles Sydney Gibbes, The Church of the Annunciation, Tobolsk, Winter 1917–18. Scan of photograph, author archive. Source: Private Collection, England.

Fig. 36   Photographer Charles Sydney Gibbes, The open carriage that transported members of the Royal Family to Tyumen, March 1918. Scan of photograph, author archive. Source: Private Collection, England.

Fig. 37   Empress Alexandra Feodorovna, "Let nothing disturb you" St. Teresa of Avila. Watercolor. Scan of card. Source: The Romanov Collection. Beinecke Rare Book and Manuscript Library, Yale University.

Fig. 38   Emperor Nicholas II, A Thank You Note to Anna Vyrubova. Scan of letter. Source: The Romanov Collection. Beinecke Rare Book and Manuscript Library, Yale University.

Fig. 39   Empress Alexandra Feodorovna, Letter of Empress Alexandra to Anna Vyrubova, 2/14 March 1918. Scan of letter. Source: The Romanov Collection. Beinecke Rare Book and Manuscript Library, Yale University.

Fig. 40   Photographer unknown, The chapel in the ballroom of the Governor's House. Scan of photograph, ID 1000010. Source: The Romanov Collection. Beinecke Rare Book and Manuscript Library, Yale University.

Fig. 41   Photographer Charles Sydney Gibbes, Liturgy in the chapel of the Governor's House, Tobolsk. Scan of photograph, author archive. Source: Private Collection, England.

Fig. 42   Archimandrite Cyprian (Pyshov), The Holy Royal Martyrs Tsar Nicholas and his family. Icon. Color photograph. Source: Holy Trinity Monastery, Jordanville, New York.

Fig. 43   Empress Alexandra Feodorovna, Troparion from the Funeral Service, 1918. Watercolor and ink. Scan of card. Source: The Romanov Collection. Beinecke Rare Book and Manuscript Library, Yale University.

Fig. 44   Archimandrite Cyprian (Pyshov), The New Martyrs of Russia. Icon. Color photograph. Source: Holy Trinity Monastery, Jordanville, New York.

Background: Volodymyr Sanych, Paper texture. Color photograph. ID: 495516172. Source: Used under license from Shutterstock.com.

Vector Ornament: Ozz Design. Vector design. ID: 70283098. Source: Used under license from Shutterstock.com.